Change
Happens:

Owning the Jewish Holidays in a Reconstructionist Tradition

Rabbi Sheryl Lewart

Acknowledgements

This book took shape with the tireless and devoted help of Miriam Bookey, whose enthusiasm and energy helped make this project a reality. Miriam, along with David Ormand, Bria Silbert, and the other members of the Jewish Learning Initiative committee in the Kehillat Israel Reconstructionist Congregation have been there whenever I called on them. I can't thank these wonderful guides and friends enough!

My friends and colleagues Rabbi Steven Carr Reuben and Cantor Chayim Frenkel, and most recently, Rabbi Jon Hanish, have been enthusiastic supporters and fellow travelers.

The idea for this book originated in KI's Strategic Plan, envisioned by Rachel Jeffer and Avi Peretz, and developed by Rick Entin, Lorie Kraus, Michael Lurey, Angela Milstein, Bernie Resser, Robert Resnick, Anne Roberts, Meli Rose, Bruce Rosen, Melanie Speiser and Moira Tenzer .

All the members of the Board of Trustees, the amazing congregants at Kehillat Israel, and most of all, the students I've been privileged to teach and learn from have made creating this book a true labor of love.

My deepest thanks go to my assistant, Mariana Grosz, for her good humor and patience.

A very special thanks to Milla Zeltzer for her wonderful illustrations. Milla first exhibited her art at The Tel Aviv Museum, as a student at an art high school. She graduated from California Institute of the Arts, Character Animation department. Her animated short film *City e-Scape* was featured in Anifest—International Film Festival—Czech Republic and Austria.

For help with the Yiddish phrases, I thank Sarah Moskovitz.

My deep appreciation goes to Christina Beausang for her patience and attention, not only to detail, but to the spirit of the book; and to Peri Holguin for his creative energy and insight.

A heartfelt thank you to editor, Melissa Brandzel, who copy proofed the text.

Words cannot express my love and appreciation for my husband, Bob, and his constant support.

Jewish tradition is a gift and a legacy, a tradition to lovingly share and pass on. I created, wrote, and shaped this book based on my personal vision of Jewish holidays and celebrations.

Stories truly take on a life of their own, and I've made my own adaptations and adjustments as I've told these stories over the years. To the best of my ability, I believe these wonderful stories were well told by:

"Joseph, the Man Who Loved *Shabbat*"
(*Because God Loves Stories*, adapted by Steve Zsitlin, ed.)

"The Purpose of the *Shofar*"
(*Kol HaNishamah Ma<u>h</u>zor*, adapted by Alexander A. Steinbach)

"The Blemish on the Diamond"
(*Jewish Stories*, collected by Simon Certner)

"A *Sukkot* Story"
(*Gabriel's Palace*, adapted by Howard Schwartz)

"A Jew Is a Lamplighter on the Streets of the World"
(based on a story by Rabbi Shalom Dov Ber of Lubovitch)

"A Purim Story"
(based on a story told by Rabbi Shlomo Carlebach)

"Micah's Dream"
(*Kabbalah Month by Month*, adapted by Melinda Ribner)

"An Iraqi Folktale"
(Shalom Hartman Institute Haggadah, adapted by Noam Zion)

"Living by Torah's Light"
(*Gabriel's Palace*, adapted by Howard Schwartz)

"The Queen's Yearning"
(*The Curse of Blessings*, told by Rabbi Mitch Chefitz)

I gratefully acknowledge and appreciate the following insights:

<u>H</u>anukah Letters Meditation, adapted from Rabbi Marc-Alain Quakinin

Tu Bishvat Tzedakah Ritual, adapted from Rabbi Rami Shapiro

Purim Flag Ritual, adapted from Tamara Cohen

—S.L.

DEDICATED

Preface

What you're about to read is a remarkable book. With gentle wisdom, poetic words of inspiration, meditations that open your heart and resonate with your soul, and stories and innovative rituals that will lead you to personalize your celebration of Jewish tradition to reflect the uniqueness of your Jewish journey, *Change Happens* is a perfect contemporary expression of the essence of Reconstructionist Judaism as the evolving religious civilization of the Jewish people.

Rabbi Sheryl Lewart is a master weaver of spiritual awareness, and we at Kehillat Israel Reconstructionist Congregation of Pacific Palisades, California, have been privileged for more than a decade to have her as our rabbi, to sit at her feet and to learn from her loving spiritual embrace. Sheryl has written a book for Jews and non-Jews alike, whether steeped in Judaism or exploring Jewish traditions, customs, holidays, rituals, and culture for the very first time. *Change Happens* is an offering of the spirit, an opportunity to discover your inner voice, the essence of your personal path to understanding Jewish holidays and traditions in a way that will enlighten your mind, bring joy to your heart, and give personal fulfillment to your soul.

We're thrilled to have the privilege of sharing this book with the world, and are confident that its unique approach to Jewish celebration will allow you to translate thousands of years of Jewish tradition and culture into the everyday miracles of a meaningful, contemporary Jewish life.

Rabbi Steven Carr Reuben
Senior Rabbi

A Word About Blessings

Blessings fill our lives. We live in a society where respect for religious freedom is a given and in an era where we can express Judaism in a plurality of ways. While we take these freedoms for granted, they have seldom been part of the makeup of Jewish society. To put it simply, history has not been kind to us. We have been isolated. We have been second-class citizens. We have been expelled. In America today, we're able to live lives as both citizens and Jews. We're able to practice Judaism as we deem appropriate. Today, we are blessed.

This sacred publication is filled with blessings. It blesses us by teaching us how to practice, how to meditate, how to reflect, and how to share. Underlying all its blessings is one message: connect. Through observance, connect with your historical past. Through meditation, connect your soul to the spirit of the holiday. Through reflection, connect the holiday's message to the needs of your community. Through sharing, connect your heart and your love for the Jewish holidays with your family and to your friends. If we're unable to connect, then we're unable to share, to love, to laugh, to teach. If we're unable to connect, we're unable to pass the wealth of Judaism to our children. This book gives us the tools to learn the most important lesson of all—connection.

Every rabbi and cantor has his or her own method of celebrating holidays (and most of us think our way is the best). *Change Happens* gives new dimensions to holiday celebration by adding tools not just to a congregant's religious toolbox but also to a clergyperson's. Step outside of your comfort zone and try the exercises in these pages. You'll be rewarded for your efforts.

Jews are commanded to say one hundred blessings a day. We're taught to begin our day by reciting the morning blessings before we even rise from our beds. Using this book will add many blessings to your life—blessings you can say and blessings you can do.

May you be blessed,

Rabbi Jon Hanish   **Cantor Chayim Frenkel**

Table of Contents

Foreword

As a rabbi of the largest Reconstructionist congregation in the world, I find myself continually consulting with our congregants about the celebration of holidays. How can we, in an authentic and individualized way, feel true ownership of our Jewish holidays as Reconstructionists? How, for example, can we derive meaning each year as we celebrate _Hanukah_? What rituals will give us a personal connection to our Passover observance?

In this book, you'll find some of the unique and spiritually uplifting ways that you, as a Reconstructionist, can observe Jewish holidays. You'll see traditional practices in a new light and approach each holiday with anticipation and a fresh perspective.

What This Book Is...and Isn't

This is not an all-inclusive book meant to give you a deep history of every single observance and ritual of the Jewish year. I won't have room in this book to tell you the reasons why the rabbis of long ago decreed that we should perform a certain act even though it's not written anywhere in Torah, or what the particular circumstances were in 1500 BCE ("Before the Common Era," the Jewish equivalent of "BC") that caused our ancestors to adopt some practices yet eschew others.

Instead, this is a book that hopes to directly speak to you as Reconstructionists who have the resources and curiosity, if you so choose, to find those answers in other places—other books, online, and other Jewish resources.

In these pages you'll experience our evolving practices as Reconstructionist Jews, with simple and powerful tools you can use to help embrace the celebration of tradition, adapt holidays for yourself and your family, and even create new rituals around the holidays while finding fresh spiritual meaning along the way.

How to Use This Book

Each chapter contains seven short sections: a personal holiday moment from my own life, a meditation, a relevant story, reflections, the celebration of tradition, "new rituals" with suggestions for personalizing each holiday, and a blessing that I've composed for each sacred moment.

For each holiday, I've created a meditation that invites you into a spiritual space where you can begin to envision, plan, and create how you, your family, friends, and community might celebrate the holiday this year. In subsequent years, as the sacred cycle of time takes you back to each holiday, you can find new insights and opportunities.

After the opening meditation, you'll find a story about the holiday. Some of my favorite stories are geared more toward family storytelling at mealtime, while others have distinctly adult themes, but all of them will provide a framework for discussion and contemplation. It says in the Talmud, "God created us because God loves stories." Many of these stories are from the Hasidic tradition where the use of stories as evocative and practical spiritual tools was deeply understood and valued.

I've written brief reflections about each holiday to help you open up relevant sacred text that are keys to discovering why the holiday exists, and why within our evolving practices we continue to observe and cherish certain rituals. Next, the section on the celebration of tradition offers the traditional prayers and rituals for the holiday. These insights about observing certain ancient rituals in contemporary times make for an ideal segue to varied contemporary practices that can serve as tools to make each holiday meaningful to you and your family.

You'll not only discover new practices that you may wish to adopt, but also participate in the process of being part of an evolving religious civilization. You'll be empowered and encouraged to search for what makes these holidays valuable and important to you in developing your own distinct Jewish identity.

You'll also find multiple places to insert your own personal reflections and traditions. The paper stock chosen for this book can be written upon, so don't hesitate to make the book truly yours by scribbling your holiday thoughts, dreams, and hopes all over it, inserting photos and recording recipes.

A Note on Usage

The liturgy used in *Change Happens* is that used in the Reconstructionist Prayer Book series: *Kol Haneshamah*, published by The Reconstructionist Press, Wyncote, Pennsylvania. The pronunciation follows current Israeli usage as used in *Kol Haneshamah*. In Reconstructionist Press publications, the "*ch*" sound (as in *hazan* and in *baruh*) is represented by an "*h*" with a dot underneath it. In this book, an "*h*" that is underlined is used ("*h*").

For a more complete explanation of the transliteration, please see pages xxvii–xxviii in the Reconstructionist Shabbat and Holiday Prayer Book, *Kol Haneshamah: Shabbat Vehagim*.

For a more complete explanation of the Hebrew texts and the rationale for offering transliteration, please see the introduction to *Shabbat Vehagim*.

The Hebrew and transliteration have been checked and rechecked for accuracy. Any errors it may contain rest with me.

—S. L.

Introduction

Reconstructionist Understanding of Jewish Holidays

A Reconstructionist understanding of Jewish holidays rests on three ideas:

1. Judaism is the evolving religious civilization of the Jewish people.

Evolving recognizes the premise that all civilizations need to evolve or die. Judaism has continually changed thanks to the survival skills we've been forced to learn, allowing us to change and adapt. **Religion** is the glue that holds the Jewish civilization together and gives our lives meaning. **Civilization** represents the type of culture and society developed by a particular group. Judaism encompasses all aspects of civilization and is not segmented from our lives.

2. Belonging precedes believing.

Belonging to the Jewish people is the key. Judaism exists for people; people don't exist for Judaism. We choose to be Jewish in contemporary society, and the challenge is to make Judaism relevant.

3. Holidays express Jewish peoplehood.

Peoplehood is a collective experience that links us through time and space. It is our common history. It is Jewish life as experienced by the Jewish people. Peoplehood is *ahavat yisrael*—a love of Jewish traditions that enables us to develop and find meaning in Jewish celebration and ritual in each generation.

And so the purpose of a book about the Reconstructionist experience of Jewish holidays becomes clear. This book explores why "change happens"— indeed, why change *must* happen. Because Judaism is the *evolving religious civilization of the Jewish people*, and *holidays express Jewish peoplehood*, we need to understand the origins of our holiday celebrations, what each holiday means in Jewish tradition, and how to make our holidays relevant today.

This is the day the Holy One has made,
let us rejoice and be glad in it
—Psalm 118

Chapter *ONE*
SHABBAT: GIFT OF SACRED REST

"Shabbat is a taste of the world to come."
—*Midrash*

Shabbat: *A Work in Progress*

Shabbat at my house is always a work in progress. Depending on who is gathering at the *Shabbat* table on any given Friday night, different traditions are introduced and shared. Some of these traditions sink deep into our hearts and remain as part of my family's *Shabbat* experience.

One favorite tradition entered our *Shabbat* space when my daughter Judy brought Jesse, a charming Parisian Jew she met in Israel, to *Shabbat* dinner. He taught us a Sephardic tradition practiced in his family (they emigrated from Morocco) when making the *motzi* over the *ḥallah*.

After the blessing, the person holding the *ḥallah* gently disengages a good-sized piece and places it in the center of the table. This piece of *ḥallah* serves to remind us of those who couldn't be at our table that Friday night. The unclaimed bit of bread during the meal evokes memories and stories about our absent family members and friends, and prompts us to talk and laugh—and even cry together.

CREATE YOUR OWN MEMORIES

Use this space to jot down Shabbat childhood memories or something that happened this year that you want to remember—maybe a precious photo belongs here.

Meditation

Shabbat *Meditation*

Begin to create your own *Shabbat* personal space of peace and rest by placing two candles on a table covered with a white cloth. This can happen on any day of the week, at any time. I find that Friday morning works well for me.

Place one candle on the table in front of your right hand. In Kabbalah, the candle on the right represents *ḥesed*, the loving kindness of creation, the gift of life itself.

Think of a moment when you smiled at a newborn baby, marveled at a budding flower, or thrilled at the birth of a new insight or idea.

Place a similar candle to the left of the first. The candle on the left represents *gevurah*, restraint and self-control.

Think of a moment when you appreciated structure, routine, and order in your life.

After lighting the candles, extend your hands out in front of you over the flames and, cupping them slightly, bring your hands back to your body, gathering the light of *Shabbat* into your heart.

Allow yourself to disconnect from the frenzy of consuming, working, and accomplishing.

Feel yourself relax. Promise yourself to find a period of time on *Shabbat* to listen to your heart, to play, to take comfort in the gift of sacred rest.

SPIRITUAL CHOCOLATE MOMENT

On Shabbat, slow down to savor small moments of love and joy. Find a moment to enjoy a piece of chocolate with full attention and awareness. Allow delight to fill your mouth. Chloe Doutre—Roussel writes in the **Chocolate Connoisseur** *that "Chocolate contains the same mood-lifting chemicals that rush in when we are experiencing feelings of love." What better way to celebrate Shabbat?*

Joseph, the Man Who Loved Shabbat

There was a poor man who lived in ancient Babylon and his name was Joseph. Next to him lived a rich Persian farmer. All his life, Joseph worked in the fields and vineyards of the rich Persian. He sowed, plowed, threshed, and gathered the harvest. The Persian made Joseph work hard from dawn to dark, but paid him very little in wages, just enough to keep alive. Even so, he still tried to cheat his employee on payday. As a result, Joseph lived a life in poverty—except on *Shabbat*.

When *Shabbat* came, Joseph was a changed man. In honor of *Shabbat*, he dressed in splendid clothes, enjoyed fine food and good drink, sang songs, and studied Torah to honor the Holy One. Everybody who knew him called him "Joseph, the Man Who Loved *Shabbat*."

As a result of Joseph's unending labors, the Persian farmer grew richer and richer. One time the Persian had a dream: He saw an old man of magnificent appearance standing over his bed. His face shone like the sun, his eyes darted lightning, and his voice was like thunder. "Behold, you oppressor of the poor! A time will come when all the wealth and property you accumulated by oppression and wrong will be taken from you, and your wealth will vanish like dust! From Joseph came all your wealth and to Joseph it will return!"

The Persian awoke, and was relieved that he had only been dreaming. But he remained frightened. What should he do, he wondered, to save his wealth from the hands of Joseph, his Jewish laborer? He conceived a wonderful idea! He went and sold all his possessions for a great sum of money, and with that money he purchased a marvelous jewel. He hid the jewel within his turban, and always wore the turban on his head. He thought to himself: "From now on, I will carry my wealth always upon me, and guard it like the apple of my eye, and *you*, Joseph, will wait a long time to get your hands on anything belonging to *me*!"

He laughed at the idea that Joseph would ever get hold of any of that wealth. "You'll still have to bow down to me for your livelihood," thought the greedy Persian in his heart, and he was delighted with himself for his clever plan.

One day the Persian was crossing a bridge over the Euphrates River. Suddenly, a strong wind tore the turban from his head. And the turban that concealed the valuable jewel sank into the river. In vain, he cried and called for help. He flung himself into the water, nearly drowning. He finally recovered the turban—but the precious gem had vanished.

What happened to it? After it had fallen to the bottom of the river, a large fish, attracted by the gleam, swallowed it. That very *Shabbat* eve, a fisherman came to the river, cast his net, and drew up that same fish. He was pleased with his beautiful catch and hurried to the market to sell it. But he couldn't get a buyer because the fish was very large and the price he asked for it was very high.

Finally, the fisherman thought of one last resort: "I will go to Joseph, the Man Who Loved *Shabbat*. Perhaps he will buy my fish. It is so beautiful a fish that it will indeed do great honor to his *Shabbat* meal to have so handsome a dish on his *Shabbat* table. Even though he is a poor man, he might buy my fish, out of love for his holy *Shabbat*."

And so it turned out that Joseph did buy the fish from him. And in the midst of his rejoicing with his impoverished family over the fine *Shabbat* fish, the youngest child of Joseph suddenly beheld the precious gem.

When *Shabbat* was over, Joseph hurried with his find to the King of Persia. The King purchased the gem to add to his own crown, and he gave a great sum of money to Joseph—whose great love of *Shabbat* brought him this good fortune.

Reflections

Judaism is a religion of holiness in time; *Shabbat* is the precious gift of time. In Biblical Israel, *Shabbat* was nothing less than a cultural revolution, the institution of a regular day off from work (freedom from human servitude).

Shabbat *Reflections*

In the Torah we read:

"Let Israel's descendants keep Shabbat, *making* Shabbat *throughout all their generations as an eternal bond. Between me and Israel's descendants shall it be a sign eternally. For in six days God made skies and earth, and on the seventh day God ceased and drew a breath of rest."*
—Exodus 31:16–17

"Let Israel's descendants keep Shabbat..."
The most important gift we can give ourselves is the gift of rest, of time to pay attention to what is really important. *Shabbat* offers a way to restore our souls, a way to heal. *Shabbat* invites us to be restful, sing songs, and take delight in creation, not to waste a single breath.

"...making Shabbat *throughout all their generations as an eternal bond."*
We become available to insights and blessings that only arise in stillness and time. *Shabbat* is sacred rest. *Shabbat* is not only the traditional Friday sunset to Saturday night when three stars are visible; it can also be a *Shabbat* afternoon, a *Shabbat* hour, a *Shabbat* walk, a *Shabbat* moment.

"Between me and Israel's descendants shall it be a sign eternally."
The practice of *Shabbat* is like the practice of taking refuge. It's a disconnection from the frenzy of consumption and accomplishment. *Shabbat* is the presence of something that arises for us when we consecrate a period of time to listen to what is most deeply beautiful, nourishing, or true.

"For in six days God made skies and earth..."
One day in every seven is biblically ordained to be devoted to transcendent pursuits. *Shabbat* is the first instance of a unit of time (a week) not tied to a cycle of nature. *Shabbat* represents the concept of sacred time. We live in two kinds of time: the linear nature of secular time and the circular (or spiral) nature of sacred time. *Shabbat* allows us to see ourselves as creators (who need to rest) as we relate to our mythic origins "in the beginning."

"...and on the seventh day God ceased and drew a breath of rest."
Shabbat does not require us to leave home, change jobs, go on retreat, or leave the world of ordinary life. We don't have to change clothes or buy any special equipment. We need only to remember—remember to play and bless, make love and enjoy food, sing and talk, and take comfort, easy and long, in this gift of sacred rest.

A BISSEL (LITTLE) YIDDISH

From Friday afternoon through Saturday, say "GUT SHABES" (Good Sabbath).
In Hebrew: "Shabbat Shalom."

Celebration of Tradition

What to Do to Celebrate Shabbat

Friday Evening at Sundown

Give *tzedakah*: Often a special *tzedakah* box is used to hold the money. What to do with the money makes for a good table discussion on *Shabbat*.

Light candles: We illuminate our lives by lighting candles. On *Shabbat*, the flame symbolizes the way we spread love in the world, knowing that our own source is not diminished as one flame lights another without being lessened.

Make a blessing over the candles:

בָּרוּךְ אַתָּה יהוה אֱלֹהֵינוּ מֶלֶךְ הָעוֹלָם, אֲשֶׁר קִדְּשָׁנוּ
בְּמִצְוֹתָיו וְצִוָּנוּ לְהַדְלִיק נֵר שֶׁל שַׁבָּת:

Baruh atah adonay eloheynu meleh ha'olam asher kideshanu bemitzvotav vitzivanu lehadlik ner shel shabbat.
Blessed are You, Holy One, life of all worlds, who invites us to be holy and kindle the *Shabbat* lights.

Bless children, family, and friends:

הָרַחֲמָן הוּא יְבָרֵךְ אוֹתָנוּ כֻּלָּנוּ יַחַד בְּבִרְכַּת שָׁלוֹם:

Harahaman hu yevareh otanu kulanu yahad bevirkat shalom.
May the Source of compassion bless all of us together with the blessing of peace.

Make a blessing over the wine—the *kiddush*:

בָּרוּךְ אַתָּה יהוה אֱלֹהֵינוּ מֶלֶךְ הָעוֹלָם בּוֹרֵא פְּרִי הַגָּפֶן:

Baruh atah adonay eloheynu meleh ha'olam borey peri hagafen.
Blessed are You, Holy One, life of all worlds, who creates the fruit of the vine.

Wash hands: We wash to purify ourselves in the small sanctuary of our homes and invoke the presence of the divine at our meal.

Make a blessing over the hand-washing:

בָּרוּךְ אַתָּה יהוה אֱלֹהֵינוּ מֶלֶךְ הָעוֹלָם, אֲשֶׁר קִדְּשָׁנוּ
בְּמִצְוֹתָיו וְצִוָּנוּ עַל נְטִילַת יָדָיִם:

Baruḥ atah adonay eloheynu meleḥ ha'olam asher kideshanu bemitzvotav vetzivanu al netilat yadayim.
Blessed are You, Holy One, life of all worlds, who has made us holy with your mitzvot and invites us to wash our hands.

Uncover the _ḥ_allah: Hallah symbolizes the sweetness and interconnected-ness of life.

Make a blessing over the bread—the _motzi_:

בָּרוּךְ אַתָּה יהוה אֱלֹהֵינוּ מֶלֶךְ הָעוֹלָם הַמּוֹצִיא לֶחֶם
מִן הָאָרֶץ:

Baruḥ atah adonay eloheynu meleḥ ha'olam hamotzi leḥem min ha'aretz.
Blessed are You, Holy One, life of all worlds, who brings forth bread from the earth.

Say a blessing of healing for those who are ill:

"Mi Shebeirach"

Mi shebeirach avoteinu
M'kor habracha l'imoteinu
May the source of strength who blessed the ones before us,
Help us find the courage to make our lives a blessing
And let us say: Amen.
Mi shebeirach imoteinu
M'kor habracha l'avoteinu
Bless those in need of healing with *refuah sh'leimah*
The renewal of body, the renewal of spirit
And let us say: Amen.

—*Debbie Friedman and Drorah Setel*

Make a blessing of gratitude after the meal—the *birkat hamazon*:

LEADER:

חֲבֵרַי נְבָרֵךְ:

Haveray nevareh.
Friends, let us give thanks!

ALL:

יְהִי שֵׁם יהוה מְבֹרָךְ מֵעַתָּה וְעַד עוֹלָם:

Yehi shem adonay mevorah me'atah ve'ad olam.
May the name of the Holy One be praised now and always.

LEADER:

יְהִי שֵׁם יהוה מְבֹרָךְ מֵעַתָּה וְעַד עוֹלָם

בִּרְשׁוּת חֲבֵרַי נְבָרֵךְ (אֱלֹהֵינוּ) שֶׁאָכַלְנוּ מִשֶּׁלוֹ:

Yehi shem adonay mevorah me'atah ve'ad olam. Birshut haveray nevareh
(eloheynu) she'ahalnu mishelo.
May the name of the Holy One be praised now and always. We praise the
One whose food we have eaten.

ALL:

בָּרוּךְ (אֱלֹהֵינוּ) שֶׁאָכַלְנוּ מִשֶּׁלוֹ וּבְטוּבוֹ חָיִינוּ:

Baruh (eloheynu) she'ahalnu mishelo uvtuvo hayinu.
Praised is the One whose food we have eaten, and by whose goodness we live.

LEADER:

בָּרוּךְ (אֱלֹהֵינוּ) שֶׁאָכַלְנוּ מִשֶּׁלוֹ וּבְטוּבוֹ חָיִינוּ:

Baruh (eloheynu) she'ahalnu mishelo uvtuvo hayinu.
Praised is the One whose food we have eaten, and by whose goodness we live.

ALL:

בָּרוּךְ הוּא וּבָרוּךְ שְׁמוֹ:

Baruh hu uvaruh shemo.
Praised be God and praised be God's name.

LEADER:
Let us become aware of God's presence.

ALL:
Godly is the energy pent up in the seed and in the soil's wondrous chemistry.

LEADER:
Godly is the human skill which brings forth food in abundance.

ALL:
Godly is our desire to feed those who hunger, to build a world where no one lacks food.

ALL:

בָּרוּךְ אַתָּה יהוה אֱלֹהֵינוּ מֶלֶךְ הָעוֹלָם הַזָּן אֶת הָעוֹלָם
כֻּלוֹ בְּטוּבוֹ בְּחֵן בְּחֶסֶד וּבְרַחֲמִים: הוּא נוֹתֵן לֶחֶם
לְכָל־בָּשָׂר כִּי לְעוֹלָם חַסְדּוֹ: וּבְטוּבוֹ הַגָּדוֹל תָּמִיד לֹא חָסַר
לָנוּ וְאַל יֶחְסַר־לָנוּ מָזוֹן לְעוֹלָם וָעֶד בַּעֲבוּר שְׁמוֹ הַגָּדוֹל:
כִּי הוּא אֵל זָן וּמְפַרְנֵס לַכֹּל וּמֵטִיב לַכֹּל וּמֵכִין מָזוֹן
לְכָל בְּרִיּוֹתָיו אֲשֶׁר בָּרָא:
בָּרוּךְ אַתָּה יהוה הַזָּן אֶת הַכֹּל:
כַּכָּתוּב: וְאָכַלְתָּ וְשָׂבָעְתָּ וּבֵרַכְתָּ אֶת יהוה אֱלֹהֵינוּ עַל הָאָרֶץ
הַטּוֹבָה אֲשֶׁר נָתַן לָךְ:
בָּרוּךְ אַתָּה יהוה עַל הָאָרֶץ וְעַל הַמָּזוֹן:

Baruh atah adonay eloheynu meleh ha'olam, hazan et ha'olam kulo betuvo behen behesed uvrahamim.

Hu noten lehem lehol basar ki le'olam hasdo uvtuvo hagadol tamid lo hasar lanu ve'al yehsar lanu mazon le'olam va'ed, ba'avur shemo hagadol. Ki hu el zan umfarnes lakol umetiv lakol umehin mazon lehol beriyotav asher bara. Baruh atah adonay hazan et hakol.

Kakatuv ve'ahalta vesavata uverahta et adonay eloheha al ha'aretz hatovah asher natan lah. Baruh atah adonay al ha'aretz ve'al hamazon.

We bless you now eternal one, the power and majesty in all. You gave us this food, you sustain our lives, through your grace, through your love, your compassion. You provide all the food that comes to us, guiding and nourishing our lives. Now we hope and we pray, for a wondrous and great day, when no one in our world will lack bread or food to eat. We will work to help bring that time when all who hunger will eat and be filled, every human will know that yours in the power sustaining all life and doing food for all. We bless You eternal one for feeding everything.

LEADER:
Let us give thanks for the covenant, for the Torah and for the land of our people's birth and rebirth.

ALL:
For the culture, faith and hope of our people alive once more in Israel.

LEADER:
May we renew our traditions, reclaim our heritage, and make life beautiful and joyous.

ALL:

וּבְנֵה יְרוּשָׁלַיִם עִיר הַקֹּדֶשׁ בִּמְהֵרָה בְיָמֵינוּ.

בָּרוּךְ אַתָּה יהוה בּוֹנֶה בְרַחֲמָיו יְרוּשָׁלָיִם. אָמֵן:

Uvney yerushalayim ir hakodesh bimherah veyameynu.
Baru<u>h</u> atah adonay boneh vera<u>h</u>amav yerushalayim amen.

LEADER:
May Jerusalem, the holy city, and the land of Israel be blessed.

ALL:
May there be peace between the children of Sarah and the children of Hagar.

LEADER:
May there be redemption for Jews in all lands where they suffer want and persecution.

ALL:
Let us strive to rid our world of hunger and violence, ignorance, poverty and disease.

Additional blessings / hopes are added here.

On *Shabbat* add:

LEADER:

הָרַחֲמָן הוּא יַנְחִילֵנוּ יוֹם שֶׁכֻּלּוֹ שַׁבָּת וּמְנוּחָה לְחַיֵּי הָעוֹלָמִים:

Haraḥaman hu yanḥilenu yom shekulo Shabbat *umnuḥah leḥayey ha'olamim.*
Compasionate one, You bless *Shabbat* as a day of rest for everyone.

On Festivals add:

LEADER:

הָרַחֲמָן הוּא יַנְחִילֵנוּ יוֹם שֶׁכֻּלּוֹ טוֹב:

Haraḥaman hu yanḥilenu yom shekulo tov.
Compasionate one, You bless this holiday.

LEADER:
Let us help to fulfill the everlasting hope for a world of unity and harmony.

ALL:
May the Eternal infuse us with the courage and strength of vision to pursue freedom, justice and peace.

ALL:

עֹשֶׂה שָׁלוֹם בִּמְרוֹמָיו הוּא יַעֲשֶׂה שָׁלוֹם עָלֵינוּ וְעַל כָּל יִשְׂרָאֵל וְעַל כָּל יוֹשְׁבֵי תֵבֵל וְאִמְרוּ אָמֵן:

Oseh shalom bimromav hu ya'aseh shalom aleynu ve'al kol yisrael ve'al kol yoshvey tevel ve'imru amen.
May the One who creates harmony above, make peace for us and for all Israel, and for all who dwell on earth. And say: Amen.

OR IF YOU PREFER, THE BIRKAT HAMAZON — SHORT VERSION:

בְּרִיךְ רַחֲמָנָא מַלְכָּא דִי עָלְמָא מָרֵיהּ דְהַאי פִּתָּא אָמֵן:

Briḥ raḥamana malka d'alma maray de hai pita. Amen.
Blessed are You, compassionate one, who provides the bread of life.
Amen.

Saturday Evening at Sundown *(Havdalah)*

As Saturday evening deepens into velvet tones of twilight, one of the most beautiful ways to celebrate is to perform the rituals of *havdalah*. *Havdalah* marks the end of *Shabbat* in tender observance inside the comfort and warmth of our homes. ***Havdalah***'s three rituals remind us of our needs for protection and safety. The end of *Shabbat*, Saturday night, is a time of transformation, a time to restore and heal our souls.

The three parts of the *havdalah* set—the wine cup, the spice box, and the multi-wick candle—represent strength, comfort, and hope. Moments of transition and change can be fearful and dangerous; *havdalah* offers sacred space and time to ease difficult moments. We gather close to friends and family, create loving memories, and wish for a good and peaceful week.

Light the *havdalah* candle and hold it high in the air during the *havdalah* blessings: This candle has multiple wicks, or you can use two *Shabbat* candles that you hold together to form one flame. We kindle a light against darkness, affirming our ability to act and change our world. We light the *havdalah* candle for hope.

Lift the cup of wine and make a blessing over the wine—the *kiddush*:

בָּרוּךְ אַתָּה יהוה אֱלֹהֵינוּ מֶלֶךְ הָעוֹלָם בּוֹרֵא פְּרִי הַגָּפֶן:

Baruḥ atah adonay eloheynu meleḥ ha'olam borey peri hagafen.
Blessed are You, Holy One, life of all worlds, who creates the fruit of the vine.

Take a sip, then pass for all to sip: From ancient times wine was believed to restore vigor. It was considered a therapeutic balm, at once healing and exhilarating. (Of course, grape juice can be used as well.) We raise the wine cup for strength.

Hold up a spice box and say this blessing:

בָּרוּךְ אַתָּה יהוה אֱלֹהֵינוּ מֶלֶךְ הָעוֹלָם בּוֹרֵא מִינֵי בְשָׂמִים:

Baruḥ atah adonay eloheynu meleḥ ha'olam borey miney vesamin.
Blessed are You, Holy One, who creates various spices.

Smell the spices and pass them for all to smell: We breathe in the scent of the spice box (or a fragrant flower or vanilla bean). Scent evokes memories. There is a special nexus, mystics believe, between our innermost selves and fragrance. Scent takes us back to the lost innocence of the perfumes of the Garden of Eden.

Hold up the *havdalah* candle: Everyone lifts their hands to see the shadows the candlelight makes on their palms. We notice where we end and the rest of the world begins as we stare at our fingernails and the outlines of our hands in the candlelight. We remind ourselves of our human limitations and yet affirm our ability to make a difference in the world.

Make a blessing over fire:

בָּרוּךְ אַתָּה יהוה אֱלֹהֵינוּ מֶלֶךְ הָעוֹלָם בּוֹרֵא מְאוֹרֵי הָאֵשׁ:

Baruh atah adonay eloheynu meleh ha'olam borey me'orey ha'esh.
Blessed are You, Holy One, who creates the light of fire.

Make a blessing of separation:

בָּרוּךְ אַתָּה יהוה אֱלֹהֵינוּ מֶלֶךְ הָעוֹלָם הַמַּבְדִיל בֵּין קֹדֶשׁ
לְחֹל בֵּין אוֹר לְחֹשֶׁךְ בֵּין יוֹם הַשְּׁבִיעִי לְשֵׁשֶׁת יְמֵי הַמַּעֲשֶׂה:
בָּרוּךְ אַתָּה יהוה הַמַּבְדִיל בֵּין קֹדֶשׁ לְחֹל:

Baruh atah adonay eloheynu meleh ha'olam hamavdil beyn kodesh lehol beyn or lehosheh beyn yom hashevi'i lesheshet yemey hama'aseh. Baruh atah adonay hamavdil beyn kodesh lehol.
Blessed are You, Holy One, who separates between holy and ordinary, light and dark, the seventh day and the six days of work. Blessed are You, who separates the holy from the ordinary.

Extinguish the candle by immersing it in wine from the cup.

Sing *"Shavua Tov"*: *Shavua Tov (4x). A good week. A week of peace. May gladness reign and joy increase. Shavua Tov (4x).*

Turn the lights back on.

GARDENING FOR THE SOUL: ROSEMARY

Grow this hardy herb to season your roast chicken for dinner.
Plant a young plant in poor soil and full sun in early summer. Invite your kids to pick some and use it as your spice for havdalah. *Rosemary awakens the senses and is often used in aromatherapy.*

Wine

H̲allah

Chicken soup

Roast chicken

Pan-roasted potatoes

Green beans

Fresh fruit and cookies

OR

Wine

H̲allah

Vegetable stock soup

Brown-sugar baked salmon

Potato kugel

Asparagus

Chocolate cake

New Rituals

Ways to Make Shabbat *Your Own*

During Shabbat, Perform Exercises for the Soul

Look for opportunities to say thank you. Each time you say it, you'll make two people happy.

Be alone for 20 minutes near the end of the day. Just sit alone in a quiet place and think of the good things from your day. Reflect. Don't plan ahead. Enjoy the moment.

Pick a single flower. Note its uniqueness. Appreciate one aspect of yourself or of someone close to you that is special, unique, or beautiful.

Treat yourself to a food you truly enjoy. Recite a blessing (any blessing that you choose) over it, before or after eating.

Close your eyes. Recall and feel the joy of doing something that you love.

Leaving *Shabbat*—a *Havdalah* Poem

Spice scent sweetness opens passageways
between nostril and mind,
tunnels between heaven and earth.

Pungent scent pierces the heavens
forcing an opening of return
for our special *Shabbat* soul.

Lent to us for the space of a day
we are loath to relinquish,
to lessen ourselves,
to return to the world of the ordinary.

In this moment of exchange,
may the memories stirred by scent
stir us and arouse us.

Familiar as vanilla in pudding or pine in forest,
or acrid wisp of smoke,
scent embraces and take us home.

In this moment of exchange,
may the scent of *havdalah* spice
open more than passageways,
may it open our hearts.

REPAIR THE WORLD: TZEDAKAH OPPORTUNITY

Shabbat *is a celebration of the gift of sacred rest. Some people most in need
of respite and rest are the caretakers for those who suffer. If you (along with family
and friends) offer to spend a few hours with someone who needs care,
it will allow their caretakers to find a few moments of blessed rest and respite.
One national Jewish organization that responds: www.jewishhome.org.*

CREATE YOUR OWN MEMORIES

*Take a few moments to jot down ideas or things you've experimented with to make
this holiday meaningful for you: recipes, something someone said that touched you,
a promise or hope that you want to journal about...*

Blessing

A Blessing for Shabbat

During the coming week
May you enjoy good health and happiness.

May peace reign over our country
And throughout the world.

May your hands shelter the candle's flame
As *Shabbat* enfolds you in respite and refuge.

May calmness replace uncertainty
As you find yourself restored in intimate belonging.

May you remember who you truly are
In your return to sacred rhythms of life.

May you take time to celebrate
The quiet miracles that seek no attention.

May you experience this *Shabbat* as an invitation
To soften and create moments of connection.

May the *Shabbat* Queen enter your heart
With lessons of love.

May you meet your beloved on the streets of Jerusalem
In the year to come.

Amen.

If you call Shabbat *a delight,*
I will make you ride upon the heights of the earth
—Isaiah 58:13–14

To everything there is a season,
a time for every purpose under heaven
—Ecclesiastes 3:1

This is the day the Holy One has made,
let us rejoice and be glad in it
—Psalm 118

You lead me beside still waters and restore my soul
—Psalm 23

Chapter *TWO*

TISHA B'AV TO ROSH HASHANAH:
SEVEN WEEKS TO THE DAYS OF AWE

"Teach me your way, and guide me in a just path"
- Psalm 27

Seven is a symbol of wholeness and fulfillment. Seven weeks separate the summer holy day of *Tisha B'av* (the ninth day of the Hebrew month of Av) and the fall High Holy Days of *Rosh Hashanah* and *Yom Kippur*. This seven-week period is known to be especially conducive to deep introspective practice and insight. Each day leads us deeper and deeper into connection with the divine spark within us. We use the heat of our internal fires to burn away our imperfections and cleanse our souls.

This minor holiday of *Tisha B'av* may seem out of step with the cycle of our personal lives. For most of us, summer is a time of ease and enjoyment of the outdoors. But our history, with its mythic dimensions, reminds us that there can be another kind of summer, one of heat as a consuming furnace. *Tisha B'av* marks the history of the summers when disaster scorched and burned Israel and the Jewish people. The destruction of the First and Second Temples, the Expulsion from Spain, the destruction of the Warsaw Ghetto— all are said to have occurred on *Tisha B'av*.

Yet the holiday turns to an affirmation of hope; in the afternoon of *Tisha B'av* we are told to sweep away the dust of our sadness and plan for a great future, one of redemption and peace. It's a custom to sweep some dust over the threshold of our doorways to announce the rebirth of hope. For each of the next seven weeks leading up to the New Year, we are to be increasingly more joyful and optimistic.

During this seven-week period, you might begin or end each day with the following prayer:

A Prayer for Awakening

I wish to examine how my life's purpose,
the ways that I can be more holy,
relates to releasing light into the world.
I accept my responsibility to help repair the world
in whatever small ways I can.
I recognize that many generations of ancestors stand behind me,
supporting my steps.
And I'm reassured that many will come after me
to continue repairing the world.
I honor all these beings as I consider my purpose
and place in the divine plan.
Amen.

Affirmations Practice

To help develop spiritual strength, one practice I like is that of using spiritual affirmations. These are positive statements that facilitate putting your intentions into action and making them real in your life. The book of Proverbs (23:7) teaches: "For as you think in your heart, so you are...." What you create with your thoughts can become your life. In Jewish Mysticism this is known as "conscious creation." Affirmations can inspire you to change your life. These affirmations are here to encourage you to use this spiritual tool to deepen your strength and confidence as you work on yourself, reflect on your shortcomings, and resolve to strengthen your character.

During the first week—from the 9th to the 16th of Av—develop your character trait of kindness.

Here are affirmations for each day of this week that help develop the quality of kindness. (At the back of this book, beginning on page **234**, you'll find the dates of all the Jewish holidays, including *Tisha B'av*, from 2009 to 2013. However, it's a good idea to get a copy of your own Jewish calendar every year so you can more easily follow and anticipate the holidays as they arrive.)

- The world depends on acts of loving kindness.
- I will look for opportunities to do kind acts.
- I will notice the kindness of another person today.
- Others will think of me as a kind person.
- One kindness leads to another.
- Doing kind acts will become a habit.
- I will be kind, gentle, and caring with myself.

Create your own personal library of affirmations for kindness. Look for quotes in the newspaper and lines of poetry. Encourage your family and friends to add their own affirmations to the list.

We can incorporate affirmations into our daily lives by propping them on the dashboard of our car, hanging them on the refrigerator, sticking a note on our computer screen. I like to stick them on my bathroom mirror or near the hook where I hang my car keys.

During the second week—from the 17th to the 23rd of Av—concentrate on the quality of restraint.

Here are affirmations for each day this week:
- Restraint and self-control allow love to flourish.
- Be deliberate in judgment.
- I will say no to a cookie (a drink, a cigarette) today.
- Others will think of me as a balanced and disciplined person.
- I will remember to count to 10 when I'm upset today.
- Self-control is the path to strength.
- I will not let my emotions cloud my mind.

PERSONAL REFLECTIONS

Use this space to note your own personal affirmations, ideas about developing kindness and restraint and some reflections.

During the third week of this spiritual time period—from the 24th to the 30th of Av—concentrate on the quality of compassion.

Here are affirmations for each day this week:
- Compassion links heaven and earth.
- Compassion inspires generosity.
- I will see the divine in a homeless person's face.
- I will move from complacency to action.
- I will really listen to others.
- I will walk the talk.
- May I reach each moment with a resolutely loving heart.

During the next four weeks, we celebrate the Hebrew month of *Elul*, considered a time to open the heart to introspection and self-evaluation. We'll refer to this period as weeks one through four of *Elul*. The day following the last day of *Elul* is *Rosh Hashanah*.

Each week, we focus on what's called a *teshuvah* practice, aimed at encouraging change and returning to our true essence as Jews. *Teshuvah* is usually translated in English as "repentance," but it really comes from a root meaning "to return," and it's this process of returning to who we really are and know we can be that marks the very personal experience of *teshuvah* every year.

To enhance each teshuvah practice during *Elul*, I offer you a daily "breath meditation" to take you through these four holy weeks. These breath meditations consist of an inspirational verse selected from Psalm 27, the traditional penitential psalm for the month of *Elul*. To do a breath meditation, simply focus on one part of the verse during the "in breath," and the second part of the verse on the "out breath." Morning is a good time to do this practice. Often, you will remember your verse and can return to it during the day. Breath meditation has a calming effect and allows you to remember what's really important in your life.

Or the meditation verse may be used simply as a focus for a few moments of quiet introspection to help you in your preparations for the High Holy Days.

During the first week of *Elul*, focus on the *teshuvah* practice of <u>Heshbon</u> Hanefesh—"Internal Accounting" Spiritual Practice.

<u>Heshbon</u> Hanefesh is a Hasidic practice that means "take an accounting of your soul." Take a few minutes every night this week before going to sleep to review your actions and reactions, the good things you did and the mistakes you made that day. End each evening's review with the hope to do better tomorrow. This practice works well when you write down your thoughts in a personal journal. After doing your internal accounting, take a few moments for breath meditation.

Week 1, Day 1 Breath Meditation

"God is my light, whom should I fear?" (Psalm 27:1)
- In breath: God is my light
- Out breath: whom should I fear?

Week 1, Day 2 Breath Meditation

"The Holy One is my source of strength; before whom should I tremble?"
(Psalm 27:2)
- In breath: The Holy One is my source of strength
- Out breath: before whom should I tremble?

Week 1, Day 3 Breath Meditation

"When enemies come after me, see how they fall!" *(Psalm 27:3)*
- In breath: When enemies come after me
- Out breath: see how they fall!

Week 1, Day 4 Breath Meditation

"Should a force encamp against me, my heart shall have no fear."
(Psalm 27:4)
- In breath: Should a force encamp against me
- Out breath: my heart shall have no fear.

Week 1, Day 5 Breath Meditation

"One thing have I asked, one goal do I pursue" *(Psalm 27:5)*
- In breath: One thing have I asked
- Out breath: one goal do I pursue

Week 1, Day 6 Breath Meditation

"Truly in a day of trouble, I am nestled in God's shelter." *(Psalm 27:6)*
- In breath: Truly in a day of trouble
- Out breath: I am nestled in God's shelter.

Week 1, Day 7 Breath Meditation

"I offer song and melody to God" *(Psalm 27:7)*
- In breath: I offer song
- Out breath: and melody to God

PERSONAL REFLECTIONS

Use this space to note your own personal affirmations and ideas about self-evaluation and introspection.

During the second week of *Elul*, focus on the *teshuvah* practice of *Hitboddedut*—"Being Alone" Spiritual Practice.

Hitboddedut is a <u>*Hasidic*</u> practice that means "being alone." Go outdoors a few times this week to be truly alone with your thoughts—enter into mental conversations of joy or anger, gratitude or pain with the Holy One. Try to be really honest with yourself in these "alone" moments.

Week 2, Day 1 Breath Meditation

"I call aloud, be gracious to me, answer me!" (Psalm 27:8)
- In breath: I call aloud
- Out breath: be gracious to me, answer me!

Week 2, Day 2 Breath Meditation

"To you my heart cries out, to you my face is turned" (Psalm 27:9)
- In breath: To you my heart cries out
- Out breath: to you my face is turned

Week 2, Day 3 Breath Meditation

"You have been my help, don't abandon me now" (Psalm 27:10)
- In breath: You have been my help
- Out breath: don't abandon me now

Week 2, Day 4 Breath Meditation

*"My father and mother have abandoned me, but You shall take me in"
(Psalm 27:11)*
- In breath: My father and mother have abandoned me
- Out breath: but You shall take me in

Week 2, Day 5 Breath Meditation

"Teach me your way, and guide me in a just path" (Psalm 27:12)
- In breath: Teach me your way
- Out breath: and guide me in a just path

Week 2, Day 6 Breath Meditation

"Don't place me at the mercies of my enemies" (Psalm 27:13)
- In breath: Don't place me
- Out breath: at the mercies of my enemies

Week 2, Day 7 Breath Meditation

"I believe I'll see God's goodness in the land of life" (Psalm 27:14)
- In breath: I believe I'll see God's goodness
- Out breath: in the land of life

During the third week of *Elul*, focus on the *teshuvah* practice of *Sheva She'arim*—"Seven Gates" Spiritual Practice.

The seven gates *(sheva she'arim)* are the openings on your face (two eyes, two ears, two nostrils, one mouth) that allow the external world to enter your soul.

Really notice each day this week how you can use your sensory impressions to make yourself feel, think, and react in positive, godly ways. Are you seeing with gates of the soul? Hearing? Smelling? Speaking?

Week 3, Day 1 Breath Meditation

"God is my light, whom should I fear?" (Psalm 27:1)
- In breath: God is my light
- Out breath: whom should I fear?

Week 3, Day 2 Breath Meditation

"The Holy One is my source of strength; before whom should I tremble?" (Psalm 27:2)
- In breath: The Holy One is my source of strength
- Out breath: before whom should I tremble?

Week 3, Day 3 Breath Meditation

"When enemies come after me, see how they fall!" (Psalm 27:3)
- In breath: When enemies come after me
- Out breath: see how they fall!

Week 3, Day 4 Breath Meditation

"Should a force encamp against me, my heart shall have no fear" (Psalm 27:4)
- In breath: Should a force encamp against me
- Out breath: my heart shall have no fear

Week 3, Day 5 Breath Meditation

"One thing have I asked, one goal do I pursue" (Psalm 27:5)
- In breath: One thing have I asked
- Out breath: one goal do I pursue

Week 3, Day 6 Breath Meditation

"Truly in a day of trouble, I am nestled in God's shelter" (Psalm 27:6)
- In breath: Truly in a day of trouble,
- Out breath: I am nestled in God's shelter

Week 3, Day 7 Breath Meditation

"I offer song and melody to God" (Psalm 27:7)
- In breath: I offer song
- Out breath: and melody to God

PERSONAL REFLECTIONS

Use this space to note your own personal breath meditations and some reflections.

During the fourth week of *Elul*, focus on the *teshuvah* practice of *Trayfe Da'at*—"Torn Mind" Spiritual Practice.

This mystical practice focuses on the things in your life that you are struggling with, things that might "tear you apart" if you let them. This week, ask yourself: "What transition point am I standing at? What is causing sharp feeling in me? Where is my suffering? What is disturbing me?" It's often helpful to journal about these concerns and take these thoughts to the *Seliḥot* (forgiveness) service, the high point of *Elul* preparations. It falls on the Saturday night before *Rosh Hashanah*. This practice should generally help you forgive yourself.

Week 4, Day 1 Breath Meditation

"I call aloud, be gracious to me, answer me!" (Psalm 27:8)
- In breath: I call aloud
- Out breath: be gracious to me, answer me

Week 4, Day 2 Breath Meditation

"To You my heart cries out, to You my face is turned" (Psalm 27:9)
- In breath: To You my heart cries out
- Out breath: to You my face is turned

Week 4, Day 3 Breath Meditation

"You have been my help, don't abandon me now" (Psalm 27:10)
- In breath: You have been my help
- Out breath: don't abandon me now

Week 4, Day 4 Breath Meditation

"My father and mother have abandoned me, but You shall take me in" (Psalm 27:11)
- In breath: My father and mother have abandoned me
- Out breath: but You shall take me in

Week 4, Day 5 Breath Meditation

"Teach me Your way, and guide me in a just path" (Psalm 27:12)
- In breath: Teach me Your way
- Out breath: and guide me in a just path

Week 4, Day 6 Breath Meditation

"Don't place me at the mercies of my enemies" (Psalm 27:13)
- In breath: Don't place me
- Out breath: at the mercies of my enemies

Week 4, Day 7 Breath Meditation

"I believe I'll see God's goodness in the land of life" (Psalm 27:14)
- In breath: I believe I'll see God's goodness
- Out breath: in the land of life

PERSONAL REFLECTIONS

Use this space to note your own spiritual practices and some reflections.

chapter THREE

ROSH HASHANAH: NEW BEGINNINGS

"The end is contained in the beginning"
—_Midrash_

Rosh Hashanah *Parenting Aliyah*

Five years ago, as our congregation grew, several congregants wanted to create a more intimate space to celebrate the High Holy Days. Services had moved outside of the synagogue to accommodate the thousands of attendees, and some people felt the loss. Now, our alternative service uses the warmth of our sanctuary as an embracing space on *Rosh Hashanah*, as congregants gather around the centrally placed *bima* for group *aliyot*.

I think the most popular *aliyah* on *Rosh Hashanah* remembers the parenting concerns of Abraham and Sarah and Hagar. I invite people to ask "for strength to be the best parents we can be, to appreciate that our parents did the best they could, and to hope that our children know we are doing the best we can."

We look at each other, and our differences fall away. We really see each other and recognize our shared concerns—that every one of us needs support in dealing with our parents, or in being parents ourselves. Young and old, families and friends gather to encircle the Torah and wrap our *tallitot* around each other in support, in connection, and in community.

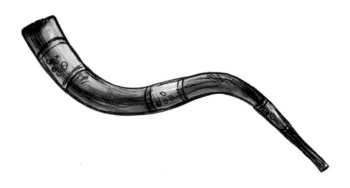

CREATE YOUR OWN MEMORIES

Use this space to jot down Rosh Hashanah *childhood memories or something that happened this year that you want to remember—maybe a precious photo belongs here.*

Meditation

Rosh Hashanah *Meditation*

Create your own sacred personal space of new beginnings by placing a white candle on a table.

Light the candle and spend a minute or two watching the flame dance.

Make a personal promise to yourself to do something important that will help you be "just a little bit better." Perhaps you'll promise to eat more healthfully, enjoy what you have more, listen more deeply to your partner.

Allow yourself to celebrate a personal moment of new beginnings.

Along with your personal promise, recognize that new beginnings bring new responsibilities. Focus on not wasting opportunities, on following through.

Think about the new year, not the old year that you're leaving behind.

Where do you want to be?

What new thing do you want to make so much a part of your life that it becomes a habit, a loving habit of your heart?

Smile, knowing that you're on your way to celebrate turning a fresh page in the book of your own life, a new beginning.

SPIRITUAL CHOCOLATE MOMENT

Enjoy a piece of chocolate in a new way for the New Year. Close your eyes and notice the fragrance. Dedicate this experience of personal satisfaction to a new appreciation of small delightful moments in everyday life. Deborah Waterhouse in Why Women Need Chocolate *says: "Chocolate will produce a sensation of mild euphoria and well-being."*

The Purpose of the Shofar

All Jews must hear the *shofar* on *Rosh Hashanah*. But it's not enough just to *hear* the *shofar*. The listener must also **understand its meaning**. What is the meaning of the blowing of the *shofar*? It is wanting to repent of past *wrongs*, of asking and offering forgiveness, and of being prepared to do something good for others.

The great rabbi, the Maggid of Dubna, once explained the importance of understanding and not of just hearing the *shofar*'s blast with the following story:

A country peasant happened to come into town one day just when a great fire had broken out. In the town square he saw people standing and blowing trumpets and beating drums, and everybody came running with axes, shovels, pails, and buckets. The peasant stood there wondering: "Strange people, these city folk. When there's a fire, they form a musical band in the middle of the town square to blow trumpets and beat drums. What's all the celebrating about?"

Someone told him that the trumpeting and drum-beating was for the purpose of putting out the fire. The peasant, who had never seen a big-city fire before, was amazed at this wonderful idea. He went into a shop and bought a large drum and took it back with him to his village.

And sure enough, one day a fire broke out in his village and the people assembled to put out the fire. He rose in the town square and addressed his townsmen: "Don't bother doing anything. It's all unnecessary. Nobody need trouble himself about the fire. I have brought back something from the city which will actually scatter the flames and quench the fire."

He took the drum, placed himself before the burning house, and started beating on the drum with all his might. But the more he beat, the more the fire spread, until the crowd started shouting at him: "Idiot! You can't put out a fire by just beating drums. The drum is only meant to alarm the populace of the village to come and do something about the fire, and to save themselves and their neighbors."

And thus, concluded the Maggid, so it is with the hearing of the *shofar*.

Reflections

Rosh Hashanah reminds us that we are created in the Divine image and that we have free will. This is a time to deeply affirm and connect the deepest essence of yourself to the sacred.

In the Torah, we read:

"In the seventh month, on the first day of the month, you shall observe complete rest, a sacred occasion commemorated with loud blasts. You shall not work at your occupations, you shall bring an offering by fire before God."
—Leviticus 23:24–25

"In the seventh month, on the first day of the month..."
In the seventh month, we celebrate and re-create ourselves as something new, something that never before existed in the world. *Rosh Hashanah* is the anniversary of the creation of the earth, the universe—and us.

"...you shall observe complete rest..."
This is a time to pay attention to what is really important, to restore your soul as a time to heal. In complete rest we take refuge in searching our souls for what is most deeply nourishing and true.

"...a sacred occasion commemorated with loud blasts."
We hear the *shofar*'s loud blasts as a call to action, understanding ourselves as partners with God in completing creation, in perfecting a world in which progress and success continue beyond our own lives and affect the world around us.

"You shall not work at your occupations..."
We stop working during this time of reflection and realization so we can see clearly how our inner being affects our performance and growth as a person, relative, friend, and community member.

"...you shall bring an offering by fire before God."
This is a time of fiery resolution for us. Aflame with our deepest convictions, we bring the offerings of our prayers and our hopes, promising to set aside all things that are counterproductive in our nature so that our full potential can be reached.

A Bissel (Little) Yiddish

Say "ZISen YOOR" (A Sweet Year), "GUT YOOR" (Good Year).
In Hebrew: "Shana Tova u'Metuka" (A Good and Sweet Year).

Celebration of Tradition

What to Do to Celebrate Rosh Hashanah

Attend the *Seliḥot* service: *Seliḥot* means forgiveness (especially self-forgiveness) and it is the work of the month of *Elul*, culminating in a mystical *Seliḥot* service on the Saturday night before *Rosh Hashanah* (unless there is a period of less than three days between *Seliḥot* and *Rosh Hashanah*, in which case *Seliḥot* is celebrated on Saturday night of the previous week). This beautiful musical and meditative service invites you to focus on where you are in your own life as you enter the High Holy Days. During this time, we offer special prayers focusing on the themes of repentance, change, and forgiveness.

Rosh Hashanah Evening at Sundown

Light candles: We illuminate our lives by lighting candles. On *Rosh Hashanah*, the flame symbolizes the warmth of connection.

Make a blessing over the candles for (*Shabbat* and) a holiday:

בָּרוּךְ אַתָּה יהוה אֱלֹהֵינוּ מֶלֶךְ הָעוֹלָם, אֲשֶׁר קִדְּשָׁנוּ
בְּמִצְוֹתָיו וְצִוָּנוּ לְהַדְלִיק נֵר שֶׁל (שַׁבָּת וְ) יוֹם טוֹב:

Baruḥ atah adonay eloheynu meleḥ ha'olam asher kideshanu bemitzvotav vitzivanu lehadlik ner shel (shabbat v) yom tov.
Blessed are You, Holy One, life of all worlds, who invites us to be holy and kindle the (*Shabbat* and) holiday lights.

Make a blessing of gratitude—the *Sheheḥeyanu*:

בָּרוּךְ אַתָּה יהוה אֱלֹהֵינוּ מֶלֶךְ הָעוֹלָם שֶׁהֶחֱיָנוּ וְקִיְּמָנוּ
וְהִגִּיעָנוּ לַזְּמַן הַזֶּה:

Baruḥ atah adonay eloheynu meleḥ ha'olam sheheḥeyanu vekiyemanu vehigi'anu lazeman hazeh.
Blessed are You, Holy One, life of all worlds, who gave us life, and kept us strong, and brought us to this time.

Make a blessing over the wine—the *kiddush*:

בָּרוּךְ אַתָּה יהוה אֱלֹהֵינוּ מֶלֶךְ הָעוֹלָם בּוֹרֵא פְּרִי הַגָּפֶן:

Baruh atah adonay eloheynu meleh ha'olam borey peri hagafen.
Blessed are You, Holy One, life of all worlds, who creates the fruit of the vine.

Uncover the round *hallah*: The *hallah's* unique shape on this holiday symbolizes the cyclical nature of life.

Make a blessing over bread—the *motzi*:

בָּרוּךְ אַתָּה יהוה אֱלֹהֵינוּ מֶלֶךְ הָעוֹלָם הַמּוֹצִיא לֶחֶם מִן הָאָרֶץ:

Baruh atah adonay eloheynu meleh ha'olam hamotzi lehem min ha'aretz.
Blessed are You, Holy One, life of all worlds, who brings forth bread from the earth.

Bless children, family, and friends:

הָרַחֲמָן הוּא יְבָרֵךְ אוֹתָנוּ כֻּלָּנוּ יַחַד בְּבִרְכַּת שָׁלוֹם:

Harahaman hu yevareh otanu kulanu yahad bevirkat shalom.
May the Source of mercy bless all of us together with the blessing of peace.

Give *tzedakah:* Find your personal way to reach out to those in need, whether it be dropping coins into a tin *tzedakah* can, bringing canned soup to your temple's food drive, or driving an elderly person to services.

Attend services.

Rosh Hashanah Day One

Attend services and hear the *shofar:* *Rosh Hashanah* is called *Yom Zikaron Teruah in the Torah,* "the Day of Blowing the Horn for Remembrance."

Wear white clothing: White helps us to connect with our essence, our inner core of purity and goodness.

Enjoy apples and honey: They symbolize sweetness, abundance, merit, and success—our hopes for the New Year.

Make a blessing over the apples:

בָּרוּךְ אַתָּה יהוה אֱלֹהֵינוּ מֶלֶךְ הָעוֹלָם בּוֹרֵא פְּרִי הָעֵץ׃

Baruh atah adonay eloheynu meleh ha'olam borey peri haetz.
Blessed are You, Holy One, life of all worlds, who creates the fruit of the tree.

At sundown, welcome *Rosh Hashanah* Day Two by lighting candles, making a blessing over wine, and blessing a new round *hallah (same blessings as Day One).*

Rosh Hashanah Day Two

Attend services and hear the *shofar.*

Eat a new fruit that you haven't eaten in a while and make a blessing of gratitude—the *sheheheyanu:*

בָּרוּךְ אַתָּה יהוה אֱלֹהֵינוּ מֶלֶךְ הָעוֹלָם שֶׁהֶחֱיָנוּ וְקִיְמָנוּ
וְהִגִּיעָנוּ לַזְּמַן הַזֶּה׃

Baruh atah adonay eloheynu meleh ha'olam sheheheyanu vekiyemanu vehigi'anu lazeman hazeh.
Blessed are You, Holy One, life of all worlds, who gave us life, and kept us strong, and brought us to this time.

SUGGESTED ROSH HASHANAH MENU

Apple		Apple
Honey		Honey
Wine	OR	Wine
Hallah		Hallah
Chicken soup		Foil-poached salmon
Brisket		Roasted vegetables
Broccoli with ginger		Noodle kugel
Kasha varnishkes		Chocolate mint brownies
Apple cake		

Ways to Make Rosh Hashanah *Your Own*

Say a prayer for beginnings:
Blessed are You, Holy One, light of all worlds;
may my life bring joy and healing to those
in my community and to the world;
may I find my way to help You
in the ongoing work of creation.
Amen.

Read Psalm 27 or this interpretive poem based on the psalm each night from
Rosh Hashanah through *Yom Kippur*.

One Thing I Ask of You

Not just one—I ask one hundred things of you.
I need not speak out loud.
Unspoken requests of my heart confront you,
demanding to be heard.

You will listen, I know.
You have listened hundreds of times before.
You know our relationship depends on it.
You hear the heart.

My urgent requests reach you by the hundreds.
You are moved, by the urgent needs of my soul.
You will let me stay with you and rest
as you have done before.

I long for your relationship in a hundred ways,
as child for mother, as beloved for lover.
I just want to look at you always,
Complete delight for my soul.

No shadowy doubts or dark despair,
bright primordial light reveals your essence.
I seek your face in a hundred places
Filled with morning light.

I feel your presence in a hundred comforts
wrapping me in confidence.
I concentrate on staying with you,
an act of will.

Be with me for one hundred days, eternity
Always with me, always.
Reassure me in hundreds of ways,
And I will finally feel safe.

REPAIR THE WORLD: TZEDAKAH OPPORTUNITY

Rosh Hashanah, *a celebration of new beginnings, is a perfect time of year
to help children who suffer. You might read or sing in a children's wing
of a local hospital. You might volunteer at schools where parents often
work two or three jobs and have no time to help the local school. Or find
opportunities that suit your skills (and those of your friends and family)
to help abused, neglected, or at-risk children and youth in your area.
One national Jewish organization that responds: Jewish Big Brothers
(and Sisters) www.jbbbs.org.*

Blessing of Letting Go *(tashlih)*: During the High Holy Days (between *Rosh Hashanah* and *Yom Kippur*), it is traditional to go to a body of flowing water and symbolically cast away your sins and regrets by tossing bread crumbs on the water. You could visit any body of water containing live fish any time during the High Holy Days to perform this ritual. Kabbalah teaches that water symbolizes kindness, and the fish (with their eyes always open) remind us to be aware of God's presence. The crumbs represent the wrongs and burdens we wish to cast away. The traditional formula on which to meditate or speak aloud is:

"If I have hurt you in any way, purposefully or by mistake, consciously or unconsciously, I ask your forgiveness."
    Or
V'tashlih bemetzulot yam kol ḥatotam (Micah 7:19)

"May God cast my wrongs into the depths of the sea. As my sins are carried to the depths of the sea, may my soul sense the presence of holiness."

GARDENING FOR THE SOUL: APPLE TREES

Amid gratitude for life itself, the first apples appear, ready to use for the traditional "apples and honey" to celebrate the New Year. Perhaps you have a protected space to grow an apple tree. Notice the way its growth reflects the shared life of family and friends who celebrate the precious gift of a New Year with you.

PERSONAL REFLECTIONS

Take a few moments to jot down ideas or things you've experimented with to make this holiday meaningful for you: recipes, something someone said that touched you, a promise or hope that you want to journal about....

Blessing

A Blessing for the New Year

During the coming week
May you enjoy good health and happiness.

May peace reign over our country
And throughout the world.

May you remember to say "I love you" at least once a day
to your partner, your child, your parent.

In only 365 days may you experience all of these—at least for one split second:

fascination   inspiration   curiosity   serenity   astonishment

introspection   wonder   suspense   solace   confidence   rapture

butterflies   bliss   peace   nostalgia   belonging   insight

humility   titillation   giddiness   generosity   triumph   awe

honesty   hope   spontaneity   anticipation   cheer   passion

pride   joy   kindness

May the spirit of *Rosh Hashanah* enter your home with blessings of love, and may you meet your beloved on the streets of Jerusalem in the year to come.

Amen.

*When the Holy one began to create the world with
wisdom, this thought, which was wisdom, created this world*
—Zohar

*Holiness is revealed in the world through
three dimensions: world, year, and soul*
—Midrash

Honey is one-sixtieth of manna
—Talmud

Refresh me with apples
—Song of Songs 5:5

Your love supports all of creation
—Psalm 36

chapter **FOUR**

YOM KIPPUR: DAY OF AT-ONE-MENT

"Look not on my past mistakes, but on the hopes of my heart"
—*Psalm 51*

Personal Moment

Cell Phone Shofar

As shadows lengthen and dusk softens the faces of congregants during the closing moments of *Yom Kippur*, the diaspora of our congregation reflects the diaspora of the Jewish people. Many of us are separated from loved ones—parents and grandparents too frail to travel, young men and women in service to our country around the world, college kids who stayed on campus.

We created a ritual that brings us all together. Instructions are given on *Rosh Hashanah* to make a phone date with loved ones. "Be ready," we remind our mothers in Florida and our children in Israel. "We're thinking of you. Please forgive us if we've hurt your feelings or wronged you in any way. We'll call you at *Neilah*, at the end of Yom Kippur, so we can listen to the *shofar* together."

On *Neilah*, as the sun's last light fades, tiny points of light glow all over the sanctuary. These lights emanate from the cell phones we hold up to capture a holy moment in time together, the great final sounding of the *shofar*. An outpouring of love, our Reconstructionist adaptation spreads community, sharing, and togetherness.

Meditation

Yom Kippur Meditation

Go on a short walk by yourself. While you're walking, look for and find a small stone or pebble.

Hold it in your hand as you reflect on your life this past year.

Remember decisions you made or things you said in anger and haven't quite gotten over.

Think of your stone as a personal forgiveness talisman.

Mentally, see yourself transferring personal disappointments, shortcomings, and failures to the smooth coolness of the stone.

Stand still and look at your stone. Close your fingers around it as you softly say, "I forgive myself. I forgive myself. I forgive myself."

Notice that you are walking on exactly the right path, the path on which you are meant to walk, your path of recognition, understanding, and forgiveness (*teshuvah*).

Place the stone in your pocket or keep it in your hand, whatever feels right to you.

Touch its cool surface whenever you need to remind yourself of what it represents.

CREATE YOUR OWN MEMORIES

Use this space to jot down childhood memories or something that happened this Yom Kippur that you want to remember—maybe a precious photo belongs here.

The Blemish on the Diamond

A king once owned a diamond of great value. He was proud of his gem and kept it close to himself. He never allowed it to be displayed for fear that some ambitious diamond thief might find a way to steal it. The king handled his prized stone with great caution. Even the slightest move could injure its pure and perfect beauty. In fact, so fearful was he of injuring his diamond that his hands trembled as he turned it and turned it, feasting his eyes on its perfection.

Sure enough, one day the diamond dropped out of his hand, right onto the beautiful mosaic floor of his secret private bedroom where he isolated this great jewel. Down went the diamond with a crash, right onto the hard tiles. To his horror, he saw a terrible blemish right in the middle of his diamond. A long crooked line marred its center!

Then the king took the gem out of hiding. He lamented to all the disaster that had struck! He consulted with diamond cutters and jewel experts. All told him the same sad story: Even if they were to work endlessly at polishing the stone, they would never be able to remove the imperfection.

"What shall I do, what shall I do?" mourned the king. "If only I had not been so selfish and kept the jewel to myself, it might be intact right now. My own selfishness was the cause of the destruction of the jewel." Believing it to be ruined, he thought, "I will never hide my treasure. Let all my people see it."

One day a diamond cutter from a distant land came to admire the diamond, which was now displayed in the public museum. Like all the others, he admired the splendid gem. "Why does the king not carve the stone and shape it into some carving that will beautify it?" he asked. "It would be more beautiful if it were carved correctly!" One of the attendants heard him say so and informed the king. The king begged the diamond cutter to tell him what he meant.

"Why, I could make your gem look even more beautiful than it was before the accident," said the diamond cutter, "if you let me try." The king eagerly consented.

With the greatest, most careful art, the cutter began his work. He made the imperfection the center of his carving. Out of the crooked line he cut out the roots and stem of a rosebud. In nature, the roots are crooked. The great diamond carver imitated the way in which a crude root, sunk down into the earth, gradually unfolds, grows into the stem, and finally produces a perfect rosebud!

And when it was all finished, the king again put it on display. Everyone understood what the gem carver was saying: Out of a blemish, out of crudeness, out of imperfection, there can come the most delicate and beautiful art. Out of a deep scratch—a rosebud! When the king, other diamond cutters, and the people saw what had been wrought with so much ingenuity, they were filled with admiration. The worst fault in the diamond had been changed into a virtue!

Reflections

Yom Kippur Reflections

Biblically ordained, the origin of *Yom Kippur* is found in the Torah. Abraham Joshua Heschel teaches, "There are three prerequisites for turning (teshuvah): eyes that see, ears that listen, and an understanding heart. If you have all three, you are ready to turn and be healed."

In the Torah we read:

"And it shall be a law to you for all time: In the seventh month, on the tenth day of the month, you shall practice self denial; and you shall do no manner of work... For on this day atonement shall be made for you to cleanse you of all your sins..."
—*Leviticus 16:29–30*

"And it shall be a law to you for all time: In the seventh month, on the tenth day of the month..."
One unique day each year, forever, personally challenges us to engage in reevaluation and change. A day of complete concentration, *Yom Kippur* is one of the most difficult and soul-searching days of the year, demanding our honesty to admit mistakes and to appeal for forgiveness.

"...you shall practice self denial; and you shall do no manner of work..."
This spiritual opportunity is clear, the ritual understood. We're invited to personally experience self-denial, to be really present to our inner selves, to atone for our mistakes, and ask forgiveness for our past failings.

"For on this day..."
Yom Kippur, the Day of Atonement, 10 days after *Rosh Hashanah*, is the last of the 10 Days of Awe (High Holy Days). Without any link to a historic event, this one day, *Yom Kippur*, promises hope and affirms the future for each of us.

"...atonement shall be made for you..."
We receive this amazing spiritual gift, a cosmic promise—"you shall experience atonement," you shall know the release of being whole, complete. I like to read atonement as **at-one-ment**, being complete and whole in potential.

"...to cleanse you of all your sins..."
A spiritual inner cleansing arises as we refrain from food, drink, perfume, sexual intimacy, and wearing leather. As we become aware of God as a source of holiness within us, the desire to atone inspires us to change. We emphasize our own ability and will to become better human beings, created in God's image.

Celebration of Tradition

What to Do to Celebrate Yom Kippur

Yom Kippur Evening Before Sundown

Give *tzedakah*: King Solomon taught, "*Tzedakah* protects from death."

Make a blessing over the candles for (*Shabbat* and) *Yom Kippur*:

בָּרוּךְ אַתָּה יהוה אֱלֹהֵינוּ מֶלֶךְ הָעוֹלָם, אֲשֶׁר קִדְּשָׁנוּ
בְּמִצְוֹתָיו וְצִוָּנוּ לְהַדְלִיק נֵר שֶׁל (שַׁבָּת וְ) יוֹם הַכִּפּוּרִים:

Baruḥ atah adonay eloheynu meleḥ ha'olam asher kideshanu bemitzvotav
vitzivanu lehadlik ner shel (shabbat v) yom hakippurim.
Blessed are You, Holy One, life of all worlds, who invites us to be holy and
kindle the (*Shabbat* and) the Day of Atonement lights.

Bless children, family, and friends:

הָרַחֲמָן הוּא יְבָרֵךְ אוֹתָנוּ כֻּלָּנוּ יַחַד בְּבִרְכַּת שָׁלוֹם:

Harahaman hu yevareḥ otanu kulanu yaḥad bevirkat shalom.
May the Source of mercy bless all of us together with the blessing of peace.

Make a blessing over the wine—the *kiddush*:

בָּרוּךְ אַתָּה יהוה אֱלֹהֵינוּ מֶלֶךְ הָעוֹלָם בּוֹרֵא פְּרִי הַגָּפֶן:

Baruḥ atah adonay eloheynu meleḥ ha'olam borey peri hagafen.
Blessed are You, Holy One, life of all worlds, who creates the fruit of the vine.

Make a blessing over bread—the *motzi*:

בָּרוּךְ אַתָּה יהוה אֱלֹהֵינוּ מֶלֶךְ הָעוֹלָם הַמּוֹצִיא לֶחֶם
מִן הָאָרֶץ:

Baruḥ atah adonay eloheynu meleḥ ha'olam hamotzi lehem min ha'aretz.
Blessed are You, Holy One, life of all worlds, who brings forth bread from the earth.

Eat a festive meal: *Talmud* teaches that "eating prior to the fast is equal to the fast itself."

Light a *Yizkor* candle: At the High Holy Days, we remember those whose love sustained us in the past and whose memories sustain us now. Remember to ask for and offer forgiveness (*Seliḥot*), even with those no longer with us—forgiving them for the hurts we still carry and asking forgiveness for the hurts we have caused. If we can do nothing else, then we should forgive ourselves for the burdens we carry. It's also an appropriate time to visit the graves of loved ones.

Recite *Kaddish*: You can find the prayer in the last chapter; see page **226**. By making peace with our past, we begin to establish peace in our present lives.

Begin the fast: Refrain from food, drink, washing, perfume, marital relations, and leather shoes.

Attend *Kol Nidre* services.

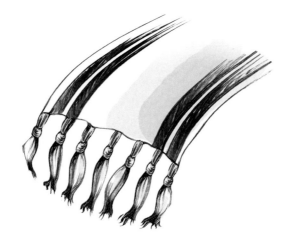

A Bissel (Little) Yiddish

At the Yizkor memorial service, or whenever speaking of someone deceased, say "aLAV haSHALOM" (Rest in Peace). In Hebrew: "ziḥrono/a l'vraḥa" (May his/her memory be for a blessing).

Yom Kippur Day

Attend morning services: Wear white. We journey from anger to healing, denial to consciousness, boredom to renewal.

Attend *Yizkor* services: Honor and make peace with those we have loved and lost.

Hear the *shofar*: The *Neilah* concluding service marks the symbolic closing of the Gates of Heaven, although the Gate of Repentance remains eternally open.

Break the fast: Do this with your congregants, your family, and your friends.

Make a blessing over bread—the *motzi*:

בָּרוּךְ אַתָּה יהוה אֱלֹהֵינוּ מֶלֶךְ הָעוֹלָם הַמּוֹצִיא לֶחֶם מִן הָאָרֶץ׃

Baruh atah adonay eloheynu meleh ha'olam hamotzi lehem min ha'aretz.
Blessed are You, Holy One, life of all worlds, who brings forth bread from the earth.

Make a blessing of gratitude—the *sheheheyanu*:

בָּרוּךְ אַתָּה יהוה אֱלֹהֵינוּ מֶלֶךְ הָעוֹלָם שֶׁהֶחֱיָנוּ וְקִיְּמָנוּ וְהִגִּיעָנוּ לַזְּמַן הַזֶּה׃

Baruh atah adonay eloheynu meleh ha'olam sheheheyanu vekiyemanu vehigi'anu lazeman hazeh.
Blessed are You, Holy One, life of all worlds, who gave us life, and kept us strong, and brought us to this time.

SUGGESTED BREAK-THE-FAST MENU

Lox, cream cheese, and bagels
Blintz casserole
Fresh fruit platter
Sliced tomatoes and cucumbers
New York cheesecake

Ways to Make Yom Kippur *Your Own*

Make "Soul Candles": A custom rooted in Eastern European tradition is to make "soul candles" between *Rosh Hashanah* and *Yom Kippur*. You can use candle-making supplies from any crafts store. These candles are unique because you make them with many wicks. Each wick represents a family member or a friend. This is a beautiful and personal way to honor departed souls at this season.

Look at the stars on *Neilah* night: It's traditional to begin to build our *sukkah* immediately after *Yom Kippur*. When we build a *sukkah*, we leave it open to the night sky. Go outside when the stars are out and the moon is visible, and stretch your arms toward the heavens. Open your hands wide and gaze between your fingers, as if you're looking through the branches that form the roof of a *sukkah*. Remind yourself that it's always possible to build a home for holiness.

Say a "Soul Prayer": Here is a prayer for *teshuvah*, change and renewal.

> O Holy One
> May I touch the source of my own strength
> To see my own actions clearly and honestly
>
> May that honesty sharpen my sense of integrity
> To face my mistakes and admit my wrongs
>
> May my strength and honesty lead me
> To try and repair my wrongdoings
>
> May courage and insight accompany me
> To ask for and to offer forgiveness
>
> May I open into humility and compassion
> To know that I do this not only for myself
> But for my family and friends,
> community and world.
>
> May I welcome God's presence on my journey
> May the year to come be sweet for all.
> Amen.

Do a Meditation of Release: Here is a meditation on the practice of *hatarat nedarim*—releasing ourselves from that which binds us.

Sit comfortably, relax, and notice your breathing…in-out, in-out. Breathe in and release. Relax on the out breath.

With your eyes closed, picture a person you know well and trust in your mind. Begin to think of all the things to which you are bound:

- My partner
- My social image
- My physical image
- My work
- Food, smoking, any substance abuse

Decide for yourself:

- This I do want to be bound to…
- This I do not want to be bound to…

Begin to think of the consequences:

- What will happen if I give up this commitment?
- What will happen if I give up this habit?

Each time you think of something you are bound to, the person you are picturing in your mind in this practice is saying *"mutarim lah"* (or *"mutarim leha"* if you are male) —you are released.

Promise yourself to stay unbound, released, free.

GARDENING FOR THE SOUL: WHITE FLOWER GARDEN

Celebrate in a white flower garden. White is the color of Yom Kippur, *known as a "white fast." White reflects the infinite and the eternal. Enjoy the ethereal quality of easy-to-care-for iceberg roses, spider chrysanthemums, and other local later summer blooms in the quiet peaceful moments of twilight.*

PERSONAL REFLECTIONS

*Take a few moments to jot down ideas or things you've experimented with to make
this holiday meaningful for you: recipes, something someone said that touched you,
a promise or hope that you want to journal about....*

Blessing

A Blessing for Yom Kippur

During the coming week
May you enjoy good health and happiness.

May peace reign over our country
And throughout the world.

May you be able to forgive yourself
And from that place of compassion offer the same to others.

May you remember the prayer of "I'm sorry"
And listen in wonder to the sound of your heart's cry.

May you follow a path that leads to forgiveness
Where you walk to the rhythm of your own inner being.

May you feel the whole world open inside you as you accept
And forgive yourself for being exactly who you are.

May you surround yourself with life-affirming companions
And dear souls who sustain all the good that is within you.

May the gates of forgiveness always swing open for you
May you meet your beloved on the streets of Jerusalem
in the year to come.

Amen.

REPAIR THE WORLD: TZEDAKAH OPPORTUNITY

On Yom Kippur, we fast from food and drink voluntarily. This time of year is the perfect opportunity for you (along with loved ones) to help fill your local food bank and food pantries. One national Jewish organization that responds: MAZON: A Jewish Response to Hunger, www.mazon.org.

Life and healing for all who walk the earth
—Midrash

When you do teshuvah, *your heart will be directed*
upward like a lily flowers with its heart upwards
—Midrash

Comfort, oh comfort my people
—Isaiah 30:1

chapter FIVE

SUKKOT: EMBRACE OF SHELTER

"We ask the sukkah to spread itself over us and rest upon us and protect us, as a mother protects her children, so that we will feel safe on every side."
—Zohar

Personal Moment

Sukkah *Soup*

Eating in the *sukkah* is one of life's great pleasures, especially here in California. We can count on warm weather, sunshine, and relatively few insect invasions. When I was raising my family in Bucks County, Pennsylvania, we had to be made of sterner stuff.

Every year *Sukkot* seemed to come at the height of the yellow jackets' final assault plans. Trapped in our small *sukkah*, we would keep a vigilant watch, hanging jars of honey water in the corners of the fragile structure to lure the wasps away from us.

When the skies threatened to open up, we would bring steaming bowls of thick soup into our *sukkah*. Sure enough, stray raindrops always dropped into the bowls. My kids were delighted with the secret ingredient, swearing that it made the soup taste even better. There was a shared sweetness in the unpredictability of the weather, our vulnerability, and the deliberate fragility of the *sukkah* itself. And, of course, we all agreed that one good thing about rain during *Sukkot* (even as we retreated to the house to finish our *sukkah* soup) was that the secret ingredient also kept the bees away!

CREATE YOUR OWN MEMORIES

Use this space to jot down Sukkot *childhood memories or something that happened this year that you want to remember—maybe a precious photo belongs here.*

Meditation

Sukkot *Meditation*

Find a time to be by yourself, seated at a desk or table.

You'll need a black marker and a large, clean sheet of drawing paper.

Draw a large circle on the paper to use as a meditative focus.

Feel yourself drawn into the endless unity of the circle.

Breathe in a relaxed, easy way and notice the circular shape of your breath, always rising, always falling.

Sukkot is spelled with a Hebrew letter *(samekh)* that takes a circular shape.

The circle symbolizes the fundamental truth reflected at all levels of Torah and reality—that there is an endless cycle to all of life, no beginning and no end.

Permit yourself to rest in this awareness of
- oneness,
- union,
- continuity,
- seasons,
- and cycles of life.

Take comfort in feeling yourself as part of a great endless circle of life and love.

SPIRITUAL CHOCOLATE MOMENT

Sit down outside with a chocolate truffle. Allow the taste sensation to fill you with gratitude and appreciation. Lori Longbotham in Luscious Chocolate Desserts *encourages us: "Chocolate boosts the production of calming serotonin. So enjoy."*

Story

A Sukkot *Story*

In the *sukkah*, the *rebbe* was enjoying dinner with his <u>H</u>asidim, his followers, when they heard a knock at the door. A couple entered, very cold and tired. The *rebbe* invited them both to join him and sit by the warm fire in the most comfortable chairs, and he had food and drink brought for them, in the tradition of welcoming guests to the *sukkah*.

In fact, the *rebbe* spent the rest of the evening talking to them. He ignored his <u>H</u>asidim, who felt left out and were very disapproving. It was not a pleasant dinner, as all the <u>H</u>asidim kept sending disapproving looks to the *rebbe*. He ignored them and concentrated on the woman. Finally, dinner over, the *rebbe* escorted the couple to the door. He came back with a huge sigh.

He said to his followers, "They wanted to get married tonight, and I would have been delighted to marry them, but you were so disapproving!"

"On *Shabbat*?!" the <u>H</u>asidim were aghast. "You would have married them here in the *sukkah*?" They looked even more disapproving—if possible.

"Yes, of course," said the *rebbe*. "Do you know who they were?"

No one answered.

Then the *rebbe* solemnly said, "Those were the *Shabbat* Bride and the Messiah. She has been looking for him everywhere and finally tonight she found him. And they came here to be married. I would have married them!

"But," the *rebbe* added sadly, "You were so disapproving. You would not give your consent!

"They would have brought peace to the whole world with their wedding. But you were so disapproving, I was afraid to even ask you."

Reflections

Sukkot *Reflections*

Only four days after the solemn holy day of *Yom Kippur*, we celebrate a seven-day harvest festival holiday, and we remember wandering in the desert after we left Egypt. During this journey, the Jewish people lived in temporary tent-like structures, simple booths called *sukkot* (the plural of *sukkah*).

The two reasons for the holiday of *Sukkot* appear in the Torah:

"On the first day you shall take the product of goodly trees, branches of palm trees, boughs of leafy trees, and willows of the brook, and you shall rejoice before God for seven days."
—Leviticus 23:40

and

"You shall live in booths seven days in order that future generations may know that I made the Israelite people live in booths when I brought them out of the land of Egypt"
—Leviticus 23:42–43

The harvest is symbolized by four kinds *(arba minim)* of trees: palm *(lulav)*, willow *(aravot)*, myrtle *(ḥadasim)*, and *citron (etrog)*. In Kabbalah, these are symbols of God's presence. Shaking the *lulav* in six directions shows that God is everywhere.

These symbols represent the seven sacred character traits in Jewish Mysticism:

- The three branches of the myrtle represent loving kindness *(hesed)*, restraint *(gevurah)*, and compassion *(tiferet)*.
- The two willows represent persistence *(netzah)* and gratitude *(hod)*.
- The palm represents composure *(yesod)*.
- The etrog represents trust *(malhut)*.

"I made the Israelite people live in booths when I brought them out of the land of Egypt..."
As distant memories of joyous harvests and festive meals in fragile huts near our vineyards and fields faded, our rabbis reconstructed the emphasis of the holiday to reflect Jewish lives in exile and the loss of independent life in Israel. Living in huts *(sukkot)* became a symbol of the portability of impermanence and vulnerability in our lives.

"...you shall rejoice before God for seven days."
Hasidim expanded the Kabbalistic idea of inviting seven mystical guests *(ushpizin)* into the *sukkah*: Abraham, Isaac, Jacob, Moses, Aaron, Joseph, and David. Reconstructionists expanded the custom to include seven women as well: Sarah, Rebekah, Leah, Hannah, Miriam, Esther, and Rachel. The custom of inviting spiritual guests, *ushpizin*, to the *sukkah* brings together our values of loving kindness, compassion, and the deep value of welcoming guests, *hahnasat orhim*.

Celebration of Tradition

What to Do to Celebrate Sukkot

Sukkot Eve

Enter the *sukkah*.

Make a blessing for being in the *sukkah*:

בָּרוּךְ אַתָּה יהוה אֱלֹהֵינוּ מֶלֶךְ הָעוֹלָם, אֲשֶׁר קִדְּשָׁנוּ
בְּמִצְוֹתָיו וְצִוָּנוּ לֵישֵׁב בַּסֻּכָּה׃

*Baruẖ atah adonay eloheynu meleẖ ha'olam asher kideshanu bemitzvotav
vitzivanu leyshev basukkah.*
Blessed are You, Holy One, life of all worlds, who invites us to be holy and
dwell in the *sukkah*.

Make a blessing of gratitude—the *sheheẖeyanu*:

בָּרוּךְ אַתָּה יהוה אֱלֹהֵינוּ מֶלֶךְ הָעוֹלָם שֶׁהֶחֱיָנוּ וְקִיְּמָנוּ
וְהִגִּיעָנוּ לַזְּמַן הַזֶּה׃

*Baruẖ atah adonay eloheynu meleẖ ha'olam sheheẖeyanu vekiyemanu
vehigi'anu lazeman hazeh.*
Blessed are You, Holy One, life of all worlds, who gave us life, and kept us
strong, and brought us to this time.

Make a blessing over the candles for (*Shabbat* and) a holiday:

בָּרוּךְ אַתָּה יהוה אֱלֹהֵינוּ מֶלֶךְ הָעוֹלָם, אֲשֶׁר קִדְּשָׁנוּ
בְּמִצְוֹתָיו וְצִוָּנוּ לְהַדְלִיק נֵר שֶׁל (שַׁבָּת וְ) יוֹם טוֹב׃

*Baruẖ atah adonay eloheynu meleẖ ha'olam asher kideshanu bemitzvotav
vitzivanu lehadlik ner shel (shabbat v) yom tov.*
Blessed are You, Holy One, life of all worlds, who invites us to be holy and
kindle the (*Shabbat* and) holiday lights.

Make a blessing over bread—the *motzi*:

בָּרוּךְ אַתָּה יהוה אֱלֹהֵינוּ מֶלֶךְ הָעוֹלָם הַמּוֹצִיא לֶחֶם
מִן הָאָרֶץ׃

Baru<u>h</u> atah adonay eloheynu mele<u>h</u> ha'olam hamotzi le<u>h</u>em min ha'aretz.
Blessed are You, Holy One, life of all worlds, who brings forth bread from the earth.

Bless children, family and friends:

הָרַחֲמָן הוּא יְבָרֵךְ אוֹתָנוּ כֻּלָּנוּ יַחַד בְּבִרְכַּת שָׁלוֹם׃

Hara<u>h</u>aman hu yevare<u>h</u> otanu kulanu ya<u>h</u>ad bevirkat shalom.
May the Source of mercy bless all of us together with the blessing of peace.

Eat in the *sukkah*: The *sukkah* reminds us of the fragility of life and how important simple blessings are.

Make a blessing of gratitude after the meal—*birkat hamazon*—short version:

בְּרִיךְ רַחֲמָנָא מַלְכָּא דִי עָלְמָא מָרֵיה דְהַאי פִּתָּא אָמֵן׃

Bri<u>h</u> ra<u>h</u>amana malka d'alma maray de hai pita. Amen.
Blessed are You, compassionate one, who provides the bread of life. Amen.

Or, if you prefer the longer version, see page 23

Sukkot Day One

Make a blessing for being in the *sukkah*:

בָּרוּךְ אַתָּה יהוה אֱלֹהֵינוּ מֶלֶךְ הָעוֹלָם, אֲשֶׁר קִדְּשָׁנוּ בְּמִצְוֹתָיו וְצִוָּנוּ לֵישֵׁב בַּסֻכָּה׃

Baru<u>h</u> atah adonay eloheynu mele<u>h</u> ha'olam asher kideshanu bemitzvotav vitzivanu leyshev basukkah.
Blessed are You, Holy One, life of all worlds, who invites us to be holy and dwell in the *sukkah*.

Make a blessing of gratitude—the *shehe<u>h</u>eyanu*:

בָּרוּךְ אַתָּה יהוה אֱלֹהֵינוּ מֶלֶךְ הָעוֹלָם שֶׁהֶחֱיָנוּ וְקִיְמָנוּ וְהִגִּיעָנוּ לַזְּמַן הַזֶּה׃

Baru<u>h</u> atah adonay eloheynu mele<u>h</u> ha'olam shehe<u>h</u>eyanu vekiyemanu vehigi'anu lazeman hazeh.
Blessed are You, Holy One, life of all worlds, who gave us life, and kept us strong, and brought us to this time.

Wave the *lulav*: Do this in six directions—up, down, left, right, front, back—drawing the lulav toward the heart each time.

Bless the *lulav* and *etrog*: Today we experience two kinds of unity, the bringing together of the *lulav* and *etrog*, and joining together with family and friends in the *sukkah*. Hold the *lulav* in your left hand and the *etrog* in your right, gradually bringing them together as the blessing is said:

בָּרוּךְ אַתָּה יהוה אֱלֹהֵינוּ מֶלֶךְ הָעוֹלָם, אֲשֶׁר קִדְּשָׁנוּ
בְּמִצְוֹתָיו וְצִוָּנוּ עַל נְטִילַת לוּלָב:

Baruḫ atah adonay eloheynu meleḫ ha'olam asher kideshanu bemitzvotav vitzivanu al netilat lulav.
Blessed are You, Holy One, life of all worlds, who invites us to take and wave the *lulav*.

Invite *ushpizin* (special guests) into the *sukkah*: Eat in the *sukkah* as often as you can during this time.

Intermediate Days

Bless the *lulav* and *etrog*.

Make a blessing for being in the *sukkah*.

Invite friends to share a meal: Whether or not you build a *sukkah*, invite others to brunch, lunch, or dinner during the week of *Sukkot*.

Invite *ushpizin*: Invite *ushpizin* (special guests) into the *sukkah*. These are traditionally the patriarchs and matriarchs of Judaism, but we understand *Sukkot* as a celebration of friendship-as-refuge; all guests of the heart are invited. Invite relatives, friends, and even imaginary guests.

The custom of inviting spiritual guests to the *sukkah* brings together several of the finest values of Jewish tradition. First among these is hospitality. Our earliest ancestors, Abraham and Sarah, had an open tent. Wayfarers were always welcome to enter their home and share their food. Consider the following as impetus for discussion around the *sukkah* table:

- On the first day, we invite Abraham and Sarah, who represent *hesed*—loving kindness.

- On the second day, we invite Rebekah and Isaac, who represent *gevurah*—the limits of being human, the fragility of human life.

- On the third day, we invite Jacob and Leah, who represent *shalom*—working for peace.

- On the fourth day, we invite Hannah and Moses, who represent *netzah*—a determination to demand justice in the world.

- On the fifth day, we invite Aaron and Miriam, who represent *hod*—caring for our bodies as a dwelling place for the divine presence.

- On the sixth day, we invite Esther and Joseph, who represent *tzedek*—being a risk-taker, daring to do the right thing.

- On the seventh day, we invite David and Rachel, who represent *malhut*—a peaceful home.

Attend *Yizkor* services: These services occur on the last day of *Sukkot* (also on *Passover* and *Shavuot*). This is also an appropriate time to give *tzedakah*.

Remember to light a *yahrtzeit* candle at home (you can buy one in any food store). It will burn for 24 hours. By making peace with our past, we begin to establish peace in our present lives.

Celebrate *Simhat Torah*: While the holiday of *Simhat Torah* coincides with the conclusion of Sukkot, it truly is its own holiday. On *Simhat Torah*, the annual cycle of reading the *Torah* (the first five books of the Hebrew Bible) is completed and immediately begun again. In the synagogue, adults and children march together with the scrolls and flags in a procession called *hakafot*. As if at a wedding, we dance with the Torah as our bride. As at a wedding feast, we take our partner, the Torah scroll, into our arms in intimate relationship and dance the night away. Instead of an intellectual learning of Torah, we absorb Torah through our dancing, and our feet learn how to walk in the path of the holy. Dance the Torah into the New Year as we dance around the *synagogue* in seven *hakafot* (ritual processions).

Ways to Make Sukkot *Your Own*

Spread a "*sukkah* of peace": For the world to change and improve, we need to be open to possibilities. The *sukkah*, a temporary "home," raises our awareness of homelessness by its very fragility. Sharing festive meals in the *sukkah* raises our consciousness of the pressing problems of hunger and poverty. The *sukkah* is open on all sides, as with the wedding *ḥuppah*. When we bring the *lulav* and the *etrog* together, we remind ourselves that the perfect wedding is possible, that the repair of the world is possible. We can bring together the *Shabbat* bride with the people Israel, two people who disagree with each other, two countries at war, two family members who don't speak to each other. The blessing over the *lulav* and the *etrog* reminds us that we need to practice openness and flexibility, awareness and goodness. Peace and wholeness are always possible. That's the essence of blessing *(benching) lulav*. The real meaning of "who spreads a *sukkah* of peace" is that it's up to us to spread goodness and openness.

Then, who knows? Maybe a couple will come to **your** *sukkah* someday, and you will be the one to turn it into a wedding canopy, a *ḥuppah* that will save the world.

GARDENING FOR THE SOUL: HARVEST VEGETABLES

In early autumn, celebrate gratitude for life's abundance with the richness of harvest vegetables that you've grown. Squash and pomegranates can decorate your sukkah. Even if you can only manage a tomato plant grown in a container, savor the ripeness of life, and in your sukkah, eat something you've grown.

SUGGESTED SUKKOT MENU

One-pot meals and casseroles are perfect for this holiday.
Hot spinach salad
Lemon chicken over rice
Fresh fruit
Brownies

OR

Vegetarian lasagna
Sliced tomatoes and olives
Chocolate chip cake

Recognize the similarity between *Sukkot* and Thanksgiving: Many Americans notice how much *Sukkot* reminds them of Thanksgiving. Our American pilgrims, who originated the Thanksgiving holiday, borrowed the idea from *Sukkot*. The pilgrims were deeply religious people. When they were trying to find a way to express their thanks for their survival and for the harvest, they looked to the Bible for an appropriate way of celebrating and found *Sukkot*. The original Thanksgiving was a harvest festival (as is *Sukkot*) observed in October (as *Sukkot* usually is). The Pilgrims wouldn't have celebrated a holiday that wasn't in the Bible. The first Thanksgiving celebrated concepts very much in keeping with the Jewish religious celebration of *Sukkot*.

Say the same prayers in the *sukkah* and at your Thanksgiving table: As Reconstructionists living in two civilizations, we can recite some Jewish prayers for our Thanksgiving celebrations.

Make a blessing of gratitude—the *sheheḥeyanu*:

בָּרוּךְ אַתָּה יהוה אֱלֹהֵינוּ מֶלֶךְ הָעוֹלָם שֶׁהֶחֱיָנוּ וְקִיְּמָנוּ
וְהִגִּיעָנוּ לַזְּמַן הַזֶּה:

Baruḥ atah adonay eloheynu meleḥ ha'olam sheheḥeyanu vekiyemanu vehigi'anu lazeman hazeh.
Blessed are You, Holy One, life of all worlds, who gave us life, and kept us strong, and brought us to this time.

Read (one or all) of the following prayers:

O Holy One, where can we find You?
We find You in the starry skies.
We find You in the blooming of flowers.
We find You in golden sunsets.
We find You in the love we feel.
We find You in the love we give.
We give thanks to You
For all your gifts to us.

———————————

For the gift of our own life breath,
For the joy of this company,
For the delight of the food on this table,
For those who prepared this meal,
Thank You God.

———————————

For the roof overhead and
The clothes on our backs,
For laughter and celebration
And the voices of the children,
Thank You God.

———————————

For all our many blessings,
For the freedom we enjoy,
To gather in any faith and language and
For the help that we can offer,
To those in need
Thank You God.

REPAIR THE WORLD: TZEDAKAH OPPORTUNITY

Sukkot celebrates the embrace of shelter. This is an opportunity for your loved ones and friends to help the homeless, those who don't have even a fragile shelter to call their own. Find about local efforts to end homelessness in your area, and find your place and your way to give back. One national Jewish organization that responds: www.nationalhomeless.org.

Personal Reflections

Take a few moments to jot down ideas or things you've experimented with to make this holiday meaningful for you: recipes, something someone said that touched you, a promise or hope that you want to journal about....

Blessing

A Blessing for Sukkot

During the coming week
May you enjoy good health and happiness.

May peace reign over our country
And throughout the world.

May you be enfolded by a *sukkah* of peace
May you be embraced by someone's loving arms.

May you feel grateful for shelter from a storm
However fragile and impermanent.

May your heart and your *sukkah* always be open
To guests you invite and relatives you don't.

May you treasure that children and grandparents
Are natural allies and that *sukkah* gave birth to Thanksgiving.

May you remember that making a living is
Not the same thing as making a life.

May the spirit of *Sukkot* enter your heart with lessons of gratitude.
May you meet your beloved on the streets of Jerusalem in the year to come.

Amen.

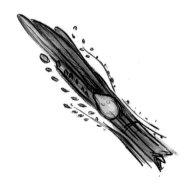

As long as the days of the earth endure, seedtime and
harvest shall not cease
—Genesis 8:22

You shall rejoice in your festival and have nothing but joy
—Deuteronomy 16:14–15

On all the days of Sukkot, you are busy with offerings on
behalf of the peoples of the world
—Midrash

Blessed shall be the fruit of your belly and the fruit of
your land
—Deuteronomy 28:4

chapter *SIX*
Hanukah: Share the Light

"The life breath of each human being is the lamp of God."
—*Proverbs 20*

Hanukah Memories

Hanukah decorations were few and far between in the stores during the 1950s and '60s when I was growing up. As a result, aluminum foil became my favorite holiday material, the weapon of choice in my childhood efforts to equalize the December holidays by making my own *Hanukah* decorations. With the help of cardboard and glue, aluminum foil could be treated three-dimensionally to form chunky *dreidels* and unavoidably asymmetrical six-pointed stars. Two-dimensionally, foil could be wrapped carefully around cardboard to create the more refined outlines of an eight-pronged *menorah*.

The ambivalence with which my parents approached the celebration of *Hanukah* was a real obstacle to my glittery foil-wrapped plans to make *Hanukah* as grand a celebration as Christmas. My parents' position as second-generation Americans, whose Eastern European parents betrayed their origins in their accents, was "don't call attention to our Jewishness."

Their position was simple: *Hanukah* was a very minor celebration satisfied by the placement of a slim *menorah* in the window, the consumption of a few savory potato *latkes*, and the rewarding of a bit of *Hanukah gelt* for the triumphant *dreidel* player.

That was the *Hanukah* of my childhood. But with the passing of the decades, I rejoice in the American phenomenon that is *Hanukah* today. I love driving around our neighborhood looking at all the lights—all the beautiful *Hanukah* lights—dedicated to those inside our home and to those passing by. As winter settles in, we light our candles and our lamps against the darkness and celebrate the warmth of communal ingathering. For passersby, our candles light the way home for those who are searching. Many of us find our way home by looking for a light burning in the window. My window is the one with lopsided aluminum foil stars decorating it—if you're passing by, come on in.

CREATE YOUR OWN MEMORIES

*Use this space to jot down Hanukah childhood memories or something that happened this
year that you want to remember—maybe a precious photo belongs here.*

Meditation

Hanukah *Meditation*

Take a few moments for yourself one evening before *Hanukah*. You'll need two candles, a *menorah*, and matches.

Take one candle, light it, and use the lit candle to light another candle, then place both candles in your menorah.

As you settle into stillness to watch the flames of the slim *Hanukah* candles dancing in the *menorah*, say the words: "Blessed is the One who creates light" *("Baruḥ borei me'orei ha'or")* three times to yourself.

It is important, at this holiday of lights, to sit and simply acknowledge that there is light within you.

Know that there is a divine spark inside you that can never be extinguished, no matter how much you are tempted to focus on your mistakes and shortcomings.

This is a time to extinguish the inner voices that keep asking, "Why did I do that? How could I have acted that way?"

Concentrate on the light, and know that God has put holy light inside you and it is there. It exists, no matter what you are doing and whether or not you are paying attention.

Enjoy these few minutes with your own personal *Hanukah* light.

Know that the light that keeps the candles glowing is the same light that will never go out in you, no matter what happens.

SPIRITUAL CHOCOLATE MOMENT

Go for the gelt—chocolate gelt that is. Conduct a personal taste test, do you prefer milk chocolate or dark chocolate foil wrapped coins? You can feel very good about Hanukah gelt consumption. As Sara Perry, in Deep Dark Chocolate explains: "Cocoa beans have a higher percentage of antioxidants than either green tea or red wine."

Story

A Jew Is a Lamplighter on the Streets of the World

There is a wonderful *Hasidic* story told of a conversation between a rabbi and one particular member of his community. The man once asked, "Rabbi, what is a Jew's task in this world?" The rabbi answered, "A Jew is a lamplighter on the streets of the world."

The rabbi continued: "In olden days, there was a person in every town who would light the gas street lamps with a light he carried on the end of a long pole. On the street corners, the lamps sat, ready to be lit. The lamplighter had a pole with a flame supplied by the town. He knew that the fire was not his own, and he went around lighting the lamps on his route."

The man then asked, "But what if the lamp is in a desolate wilderness?" The rabbi responded, "Then, too, one must light it."

Not satisfied, the man asked, "But what if the lamp is in the middle of the sea?" to which the rabbi responded, "Then the lamplighter must take off his clothes, jump into the water, and light it there!"

"And *that* is the Jew's mission?" asked the man. The rabbi thought for a long moment and finally responded, "Yes, that is a Jew's calling." The man persisted: "But rabbi, I see no lamps." The rabbi responded, "That is because you are not yet a lamplighter." "So," the man inquired, "how does one become a lamplighter?"

The rabbi's answer this time? "One must begin with oneself, cleansing oneself, becoming more refined. Then one is able to see the other as a source of light, waiting to be ignited. When your soul burns with the light of kindness and compassion, then you can see others longing to burst into light, yearning to help illumine and warm the world. You become a lamplighter—one who lights the hearts and souls of others."

Reflection

Hanukah is different from all other Jewish holidays and festivals because it is the first festival created by the Jewish people. It is not mentioned in the Torah. In the verse from the Book of Numbers, the *menorah* is used in the Temple and has only seven lights.

A Hanukah *Reflection*

In the Oxford Bible, we read:

"Celebrate the purification of the Temple—also the festival of the kindling of the fire."
—2 Maccabees 1:18–19

In the Torah, we read:

"When you go up to the lights, let the lights give light on the face of the menorah."
—Numbers 8:2

"Celebrate the purification of the Temple..."
At the darkest time of the year, we light candles to celebrate the story of the Maccabees. The story is usually told that when the Hellenized Syrian rulers of Israel forbade the practice of Judaism, an uprising began in the hills around Modi'in. The priest Mattityahu and his sons—the Maccabees, as they were called—defeated the Syrians against all odds. When they cleaned and restored the Temple in Jerusalem, they managed to light the great *menorah*. Somehow, miraculously, the light lasted eight days. Ever since, we celebrate *Hanukah* (which means "dedication" in Hebrew) by lighting candles for eight days.

"...also the festival of the kindling of the fire."
The two themes of *Hanukah*—the miracle of the oil and the victory of the few against the many—have shifted in emphasis and importance back and forth over time. The rabbis who preserved Judaism for us after the Roman conquest of Israel (think of Masada) wanted no holidays celebrating rebellion against authority after the defeat of Bar Kochba and the warlike advice of Rabbi Akiba. Having seen their people's insurrections against Rome end in wholesale slaughter and the end of the Jewish state, they were not anxious to glorify militarism. They counseled Jews to act like a reed and bend, rather than break, and decided to exclude the books of First and Second *Maccabees* from the Torah. They added the miracle of the small vial of oil that burned for eight days.

Hanukah was observed for 600 years before the Talmud explained "Why do we celebrate *Hanukah*?" as a celebration of the miracle of the jar of oil that burned for eight nights. No Judah, no rebellion, no guerilla warriors, but salvation by God and a small miracle. The rabbis added the *haftorah* of Zachariah to emphasize the point "not by strength, not by power, but by My might, says the Lord of Hosts." The holiday of human triumph against resistance became one more instance of waiting patiently for God to save the Jews.

"When you go up to the lights..."
In medieval times, the need for a miracle was uppermost on Jewish minds as the senseless and relentless path of death cut by the Crusaders' swords swept across Europe. The martyrdom story of Hannah and her seven sons was the *Hanukah* inspiration of the Jewish medieval mindset.

As the State of Israel began to birth itself at the beginning of the 20th century, *Hanukah* emerged as a military celebration of guerilla tactics and cunning victories wrestled from the hands of a strong enemy. The Zionists had found a hero in Jewish tradition: Judah the Maccabee. To this day, Israeli children run around with plastic hammers (*maccabee* means "hammer") and celebrate *Hanukah* by banging on everything and everyone as they munch on *sufganiyot* (sugared donuts).

In the United States, we have created a strong alternative to the Christmas celebrations that wrap this country as a giant gifting experience. We focus on our Jewish identity and the call for the few to stand up against the many.

"...let the lights give light..."
We remember *Hanukah* as a time of dedication, and it survives to celebrate the right of all individuals to their own character and identity. It offers us a chance to spread our own sparks of divine light at this season of light, and dedicate ourselves and our families to making the world a better place as we repair ourselves *(tikkun hanefesh)* and repair the world *(tikkun olam)*.

"...on the face of the menorah..."
And let's not forget that *Hanukah* stands as a great example of Reconstructionist process, of reconsidering and reconstructing an ancient tradition to meet the needs of our people in our time. We have always celebrated *Hanukah* because we find it meaningful and relevant to our lives, not because we read in the Torah that we should observe this festival. *Hanukah* is truly a Reconstructionist holiday. Throughout its long history of celebration it has been re-created and reinvented, redefined—and, yes, reconstructed—to respond to the needs of the Jewish people in different eras.

Reflections on the "Light of Hanukah"

Some 2,000 years ago, the rabbis of the Talmud invited us to focus on the lights and spend precious moments in reflection of the light we bring into the world. In answering the question "What is *Hanukah*?" the rabbis remind us that unlike any other lights we kindle during the year—whether on *Shabbat* or other holidays—on *Hanukah* the lights are kindled for the sole purpose of noticing the light. This light is not to read by or to light our way in a dark room, but solely for reflecting on what it means to bring light into our world and how we can be a part of that process. In the words of one of the traditional meditative readings that accompany the blessings over the candles: "*Haneirot Hallalu*—these lights we kindle for the miracles, for the wonders. And throughout the eight days of *Hanukah* these lights are sanctified...and we do not have the permission to use them except to look at them."

Yet, whenever it is that we return from our day and light our *Hanukah* candles, there are so many other things to do—gifts to exchange, dinners to eat, work to be done, a household to run. They are things that distract us from sitting and watching the burning flames of our *Hanukah* lights. As a result, although the lights of our *menorah* burn brightly each night, it's so easy to ignore or forget the light of the *menorah* and all that it has to share with us.

Each night's candles will burn until all that is left is each small wick of flames desperately trying to continue to revive itself as it starts to burn low. And inevitably, sad as it may be, it will eventually burn out. And what will we do? The next night, we will not only relight that candle, but we will add more light to the *menorah*, increasing the light shining from our homes. And so, too, will we do so for each of the eight nights of *Hanukah*.

A BISSEL (LITTLE) YIDDISH

The dreidel *game really works in Yiddish. On the* dreidel, *the Yiddish letters on the* dreidel *tell you how to play:* Nem *(take),* Gib *(give),* Halb *(half), and* Shtel *(put all). In Hebrew the letters stand for* Nes Gadol Hayyah Sham *(A Great Miracle Happened There). In Israel today, the letters on the* dreidel *have been changed to* Nes Gadol Hayyah Po *(A Great Miracle Happened Here).*

Lighting the _Hanukah_ menorah invites us to ignite the flames of our own souls, to find the spark that cannot be extinguished, the spark that can burn not just for eight days, but for the entire year. As the light of our _menorah_ burns, our internal light must also be kindled in the fight against darkness of evil and indifference.

The _menorah_ reminds us of the miracle that no matter how dark life may be, hope and faith can inspire a source of light deep within each of us. And it reminds us that the light of our soul reflects and refracts God's illuminating presence—in the words of Proverbs, "The light of God is the human soul." It is this light that can also lead our way and illumine our darkest path. And it is this light that we can use to kindle other holy lights—the souls within others around us.

Celebration of Tradition

What to Do to Celebrate <u>H</u>anukah

Light the candles: Candles are lit after dark. It is traditional to place the candles in a window where they can be seen from the street. On Friday evening, the <u>Hanukah</u> candles are lit prior to lighting the *Shabbat* candles.

Take care with order: When placing candles in the *menorah*, we start on the right, putting in one candle for each night, plus the *shamash* or "servant" candle. After the blessings are recited, we use the *shamash* to light the other candles from left to right.

Bless the candles:
First, say:

בָּרוּךְ אַתָּה יהוה אֱלֹהֵינוּ מֶלֶךְ הָעוֹלָם, אֲשֶׁר קִדְּשָׁנוּ
בְּמִצְוֹתָיו   וְצִוָּנוּ לְהַדְלִיק נֵר שֶׁל חֲנֻכָּה׃

Baru<u>h</u> atah adonay, eloheynu mele<u>h</u> ha'olam, asher kideshanu bemitzvotav vetzivanu, lehadlik ner shel <u>H</u>anukah.
Blessed are You, Holy One, life of all worlds, who invites us to be holy and kindle the *<u>Hanukah</u>* lights.

Second, say:

בָּרוּךְ אַתָּה יהוה אֱלֹהֵינוּ מֶלֶךְ הָעוֹלָם שֶׁעָשָׂה נִסִּים
לַאֲבוֹתֵינוּ בַּיָּמִים הָהֵם בַּזְּמַן הַזֶּה׃

Baruh atah Adonay, eloheynu meleh ha'olam, sheh'asah nissim la'avoteynu, bayamim haheim, bazeman hazeh.
Blessed are You, Holy One, life of all worlds, who performed miracles for our ancestors at this season in ancient days.

On the first night only, include the *sheheheyanu*:

בָּרוּךְ אַתָּה יהוה אֱלֹהֵינוּ מֶלֶךְ הָעוֹלָם שֶׁהֶחֱיָנוּ וְקִיְּמָנוּ
וְהִגִּיעָנוּ לַזְּמַן הַזֶּה׃

Baruh atah adonay eloheynu meleh ha'olam sheheheyanu vekiyemanu vehigi'anu lazeman hazeh.
Blessed are You, Holy One, life of all worlds, who gave us life, and kept us strong, and brought us to this time.

SUGGESTED HANUKAH MENU

Cucumber salad
Brisket
Potato latkes with applesauce
Broccoli
Lemon mousse pie
Doughnuts (sufganiyot)

OR

Mushroom soup
Southwestern grilled salmon
Potato/zucchini latkes
Dark chocolate cheesecake

New Rituals

Ways to Make <u>H</u>anukah *Your Own*

Use the lighting of the candles as a gratitude practice.
The Talmud says, "All the darkness cannot extinguish the light of a single candle, yet one candle can illuminate all the darkness."

First candle: Create a family or group blessing together. Hang it on the refrigerator for the rest of *Hanukah*.

Second candle: Pay close attention to the household tasks of sharing a meal with each other. Focus your attention on each part of preparation, presentation, and cleanup. Think about how fortunate you are to have enough to eat. Think of those who do not. Make a promise to help serve a meal at a homeless shelter or send money to MAZON, a nonprofit organization that confronts hunger in the U.S. and around the world.

Third candle: Make a pledge to reverse any tendency you have to make comparisons. Quit talking about what you don't have compared to what you do have. Cultivate an "attitude of gratitude" tonight.

Fourth candle: Light a candle for gratitude and dedicate it to people you know, or people you don't know but admire (living or dead). *Hanukah* recounts the story of a small ragtag band of rural Jews, the Maccabees, and their victory over the Syrian-Greek military machine and the Hellenistic repression. It is called the "Festival of Lights" because of the legend of the small vial of oil that burned for eight days during the rededication of the Second Temple in Jerusalem by Judah and his *Maccabees*. *Hanukah* means "dedication," not only by historic reference, but as an opportunity for us to make personal dedications and resolutions. It is truly a joyous time of year!

GARDENING FOR THE SOUL: POTATOES

There is a need to appreciate the humble potato. An easy-to-grow vegetable, potatoes can rest in the ground for a long time (even until December in warm climates). If you've dug them up, place them in a cool, dry space and use them for your **latkes***. Be daring: Try sweet potatoes, too, if your climate allows. A potato plant is a pretty asset to any garden.*

Fifth candle: Create a "gratitude calendar." Set up a schedule of blessing emphases in a datebook, perhaps having a different focus for each month: service providers, places, animals, nature are a few ideas. Create your own list of 12.

Sixth candle: Do a survey of your possessions and give away those things that you no longer use or cherish. If you are not grateful for them, give them to someone who would appreciate them.

Seventh candle: Recall a place in your life that you have had to let go of, and then express gratitude for what it was to you for a while.

Eighth candle: Tell two people why you are grateful that they are in your life.

Use the lighting of the candles as a personal meditation practice

A thought for each night: Each night of _Hanukah_ is numbered one through eight. In Hebrew, these numbers appear as the letters _alef, bet, gimmel, dalet, heh, vav, zayin,_ and _het_, and each night offers an opportunity to enter a "gate."

The Gate of _Alef_
The symbol of the _alef_ (the letter originally looked like a circle with horns) is the head of an ox, which was used to pull plows to turn the earth. In effect, we are the earth, the way earth knows itself and God. If the soil is not turned, however, it becomes hard-packed and no longer capable of bringing forth life. We turn the soil of self through spiritual practice. As you enter the Gate of _alef_, ask where you need turning—and what you can you do to release the healing creativity that is your true nature.

The Gate of _Bet_
This is the place of intimacy with yourself and others. The _bet_ is closed on three sides. Your history (the back), your birth (the bottom), and your death (the top) are closed—you cannot escape your biology, the things you've done, your mortality. Only the present is open to you. As you enter this gate, ask where you are wasting energy—and how you can refocus on things you can control.

The Gate of _Gimmel_
The sign of the _gimmel_ (originally a figure of a _gamal_, or camel) represents your ability to cross deserts—those times of barrenness, dryness, lack of creativity. Such times are often the most spiritually healing. See if you can hear—as Hosea did—God's voice saying, "I will call you to the desert and there I will speak to your heart."

The Gate of *Dalet*

Dalet represents the doors of life you walk through and which close behind you. Ask which door is waiting for you to walk through. Walk on. Enter your doorway.

The Gate of *Heh*

This letter, originally written with two vertical lines extended on both sides above the top horizontal line, was the sign of a person in prayer. As you enter this gate, think about a state when you felt holiness, awe, and wonder—and what you might do to invite that state once more.

The Gate of *Vav*

This Gate of Connection (the original *vav* was the symbol of a nail) reflects that all things are part of the One that is God. As you enter this gate, ask where you are forcing connections, nailing things together, when—if approached wisely—they would fit together like pieces of a jigsaw puzzle.

The Gate of *Zayin*

The sign of the arrow (the original letter *zayin*) makes this the Gate of Conflict, which is natural to life and neither good nor bad. At this gate, examine conflicts in your life—whether you are wrestling or dancing—and what you might do to dance a bit more.

The Gate of *Het*

Het, originally the symbol of an enclosure, or pen, is your ability to hold things. As you enter this gate, consider whether your life is defined by "either/or" or "both/and." What can you do to expand your capacity to hold?

REPAIR THE WORLD: TZEDAKAH OPPORTUNITY

Hanukah, when we dedicate ourselves to "share the light," offers you (and your friends and family) the opportunity to provide warm clothing and blankets for those who are struggling to survive the harshness of a winter lived in poverty. One national Jewish organization that responds: National Jewish Outreach Program, www.njop.org.

PERSONAL REFLECTIONS

Take a few moments to jot down ideas or things you've experimented with to make this holiday meaningful for you: recipes, something someone said that touched you, a promise or hope that you want to journal about….

Blessing

A Blessing for <u>Hanukah</u>

May this season of light be filled with blessings
May you kindle your own inner light
And be a lamplighter for others
May you further the act of creation and re-creation
Acknowledging your partnership with the Holy.

As each candle represents one of the 36 souls
that guard the world
May you become a guardian of the world at *<u>Hanukah</u>*.
May you sustain, nurture, and guard this light.

May you recognize that within you are sparks of hidden light
With the power to transform
And illuminate and heal.
<u>Hanukah</u> lights are holy, a beacon
That darkness can be dispelled with wisdom
Obscurity can be illuminated with truth.

<u>Hanukah</u> lights are hope—the hope that
Redemption will happen
That light will triumph over negativity.
You are the guardian—you are the hope.

Amen.

Dance before the lamps with burning torches
in their hands, singing songs
—Talmud

I desire to create the world with light
—Midrash

Let the lamps give light
—Numbers 8:2

To a candle that was burning, one lit from it many other
candles, yet the light of its flame did not diminish,
so too give of your spirit and lose nothing of your own
—Midrash

chapter SEVEN

TU BISHVAT: TREES OF LIFE

"A person is like a tree of the field...a tree in the Holy Apple Orchard that is the Sheḥinah."

—*Zohar*

Personal Moment

Tu Bishvat Seder

Everyone in the adult *b'nai mitzvah* class was excited about sharing a *Seder* together in January. We had studied the mystical basis of the *Tu Bishvat Seder*—that the New Year of the Trees represents the Tree of Life in the Torah. We planned a *Seder* honoring Kabbalah's four worlds as the mystics in Safed did 500 years ago.

Two women members of the class, an artist and a decorator, created a spectacular setting. Four round tables were arrayed with tablecloths in all white, pale pink, rose, and deep wine red to represent the four worlds: winter, spring, summer, and fall. Candles shimmered and glowed, and flowers and mirrors completed the *Seder* tables.

Just moments before everyone was to gather, we noticed that the food was missing. Carefully chosen and arranged platters of fruits, nuts, and chocolates had disappeared from the KI kitchen. Dismayed, we realized that religious school teachers had mistakenly used the food for the school's *Tu Bishvat Seder*! Some of us raced to the grocery store and filled two shopping carts with everything we could remember—fruits with no seeds, fruits with seeds...with hard shells, with no shells...and, of course, chocolate. The *Seder* went off without a hitch, and we all agreed that even the Tree of Life has unexpected twists in her branches.

CREATE YOUR OWN MEMORIES

*Use this space to jot down Tu Bishvat (or celebrations in Nature) childhood memories
or something that happened this year that you want to remember—
maybe a precious photo belongs here.*

Meditation

A Tu Bishvat *Meditation*

Go and meditate in a garden, a forest, someplace where you can enjoy the beauty of a tree.

Settle into stillness, feel yourself rooted in place. Notice the ground beneath your feet.

Recognize that within you, as well as within a tree, there is a flowing energy, an inner nourishment that allows you to flourish.

Promise to do all you can to nurture yourself, to care for yourself.

Take your own physical health and well-being seriously.

Have you been eating well? Sleeping well?

Do you feel static or stuck?

Think of energy flowing through your body, like sap inside a tree, rising and filling you with exactly what you need.

Think of yourself as a Tree of Life, trusting that the care you take of yourself will pay off for you.

SPIRITUAL CHOCOLATE MOMENT

An Aztec legend recounts that from the realm of the Sun God, from Paradise itself, Quetzalcoatl, returned to the world of humanity with cacao seeds in his hands. Chocolate is the food of the gods. Savor a chocolate moment as the highest level of taste satisfaction. Trust your awareness that chocolate is a divine food.

Micah's Dream

Once, many years ago, there lived a Jew named Micah who had a dream of world peace. He built a special house to reflect his dream. His house was built out of stone because he did not want to destroy any trees in the building of his house. He also did not want to use metal tools to carve the stones, for metal tools can be used as weapons that destroy life. So he built it all with his own hands, like the altar in the Holy Temple. He then planted a fig tree outside of his house and placed a table in its shade.

Like the Holy Temple, he envisioned his house as a place for all people. People would visit him from everywhere and he would feed them under the fig tree. He would leave the crumbs remaining from the meals and the birds would fly down to eat them. Micah, of course, was a vegetarian, an ardent one.

One day a prophet visited Micah, though Micah did not know that the man was a prophet. After staying in Micah's house for a few days, he said that he had to leave and wanted to pay him. Micah did not want to take money for his hospitality, but he did not want to make a big fuss in front of the man, so he accepted it and then slipped the money back into the pocket of the prophet's coat.

The prophet, however, knew what Micah had done and gave him a blessing. He said to Micah, "In heaven they are so impressed with your house. I'm here to tell you that one day a child of yours will eat a fig from the tree outside of your house and this will bring the Messianic days—*yemai hamashiah*."

Micah did not have any children at that time.

The next day the Romans invaded Jerusalem. They destroyed the Temple and Micah's home. Micah went into exile along with many other Jews. But the dream of Micah and his story continue to be told to this day.

For thousands of years, and even today, people have been serving figs to their children, because maybe, just maybe, one of their children is a child of Micah—and maybe, just maybe, one of these figs is from a tree that grew from a seed of another tree that can be traced back to Micah's fig tree. So one day, the prophet's words may come true: that the Messianic times will indeed come when one of Micah's descendants eats a fig of Micah's tree.

Reflections

Tu Bishvat *Reflections*

We are part of an interconnected, interdependent, universal web of life. In Israel at *Tu Bishvat* (the 15th day of the month of *Shevat*), most of the winter rains are over and the sap begins to rise in the trees. The holiday, observed at the full moon of midwinter, saw ancient tax collectors and orchard keepers choose this moment in time to mark the beginning of a new growing year. That is why *Tu Bishvat* is also called "the New Year of Trees" in Jewish tradition.

In the Bible we read:

"There is hope for a tree; if it is cut down it will renew itself;
Its shoots will not cease.
If its roots are old in the earth,
And its stump dies in the ground,
At the scent of water it will bud
And produce branches like a sapling."
—Job 14:7–9

"There is hope for a tree; if it is cut down it will renew itself;"
Sixteenth-century mystics, unable to own land, turned to an interior landscape planted with Torah, the Tree of Life. They reconstructed the holiday as a time to examine the fruit of our personal Tree, the Tree of (your) Life.

A BISSEL (LITTLE) YIDDISH

On Tu Bishvat, LOMIR SHPATSIRN *(Let's Take a Walk). To every greeting, no matter what it is, you can always answer,* "GIT YOOR" *(A Good Year). In Hebrew, you can respond to almost any greeting with* "Gam Leha" *(And to you).*

"Its shoots will not cease."
The flow of life and energy from God was pictured by the Kabbalists as coming through the Divine Tree, another "Tree of Life," as they called it. This life-giving cosmic Tree of Life is inverted: Its roots are in the heavens with God, invisible, inexplicable, unknowable, yet its branches stretch down toward us, bringing the flow of God's energy that creates, shapes, and gives life to our world.

"If its roots are old in the earth,
And its stump dies in the ground,"
Israeli tree planters and American Jews refocused the holiday on the dangers that today threaten not only forests, but also many of the natural habitats around our fragile planet.

"At the scent of water it will bud
And produce branches like a sapling."
Tu Bishvat invites us to celebrate and reflect on all our relationships with trees: the fruit-giving trees of the *Mishnah* and the replanted national trees of Israel, and the universal, life-giving global trees of the ecosphere and the cosmic Tree of Kabbalah.

Celebration of Tradition

What to Do to Celebrate Tu Bishvat

Observed at the full moon of midwinter, *Tu Bishvat* was started by ancient tax collectors and orchard keepers to mark the beginning of a new growing year. A portion of the fruit produced in that year was set aside as a tithe. Sixteenth-century mystics created a holiday based on these traditions, and, in turn, Israeli tree planters and American Jews have refocused the holiday on the dangers that today beset not only forests, but also many of the natural habitats around our fragile planet.

Host a *Tu Bishvat Seder:* Here is a *Haggadah* for The Festival of Trees.

1. CREATION: WINTER

Pour the first cup: This cup is white wine or juice.

Serve the first fruit: This fruit should have a hard outer shell but a soft inner shell (pomegranate, walnut, coconut, pineapple).

Make a blessing of gratitude—the *sheheḥeyanu:*

בָּרוּךְ אַתָּה יהוה אֱלֹהֵינוּ מֶלֶךְ הָעוֹלָם שֶׁהֶחֱיָנוּ וְקִיְמָנוּ
וְהִגִּיעָנוּ לַזְּמַן הַזֶּה:

Baruḥ atah adonay eloheynu meleḥ ha'olam sheheḥeyanu vekiyemanu vehigi'anu lazeman hazeh.
Blessed are You, Holy One, life of all worlds, who gave us life, and kept us strong, and brought us to this time.

Make a blessing over the wine—the *kiddush:*

בָּרוּךְ אַתָּה יהוה אֱלֹהֵינוּ מֶלֶךְ הָעוֹלָם בּוֹרֵא פְּרִי הַגָּפֶן:

Baruḥ atah adonay eloheynu meleḥ ha'olam borey peri hagafen.
Blessed are You, Holy One, life of all worlds, who creates the fruit of the vine.

Make a blessing over the fruit of the earth:

בָּרוּךְ אַתָּה יהוה אֱלֹהֵינוּ מֶלֶךְ הָעוֹלָם בּוֹרֵא פְּרִי הָאֲדָמָה:

Baruḥ atah adonay eloheynu meleḥ ha'olam borey peri h'adamah.
Blessed are You, Holy One, life of all worlds, who creates the fruit of the earth.

Reading:

On this day, when we celebrate the renewal of trees, we remember that God created all plants and trees. Then God said, "See, I give you every seed-bearing plant that is upon all the earth, and every tree that is upon all the earth, and every tree that has seed-bearing fruit; they shall be yours for food." And it was so.
—*Genesis 1:29–31*

2. RENEWAL: SPRING

Pour the second cup: This cup is blush (white with red) wine or juice.

Serve the second fruit: This fruit should have a soft outer shell but a hard inner seed (olive, avocado, cherry, peach, date).

Make a blessing over the wine—the *kiddush*:

בָּרוּךְ אַתָּה יהוה אֱלֹהֵינוּ מֶלֶךְ הָעוֹלָם בּוֹרֵא פְּרִי הַגָּפֶן׃

Baruḥ atah adonay eloheynu meleḥ ha'olam borey peri hagafen.
Blessed are You, Holy One, life of all worlds, who creates the fruit of the vine.

Make a blessing over the fruit of the earth:

בָּרוּךְ אַתָּה יהוה אֱלֹהֵינוּ מֶלֶךְ הָעוֹלָם בּוֹרֵא פְּרִי הָאֲדָמָה׃

Baruḥ atah adonay eloheynu meleḥ ha'olam borey peri ha'adamah.
Blessed are You, Holy One, life of all worlds, who creates the fruit of the earth.

Responsive reading:

The fruits which nourish life come from the trees of God's earth.

Torah, which is a Tree of Life, comes from our covenant with God.

We celebrate the trees which give us fruit. We celebrate Torah, the Tree of Life, which nourishes the spirit.

On *Tu Bishvat* we celebrate the Divine Tree of Life, and the renewal of the flow of God's creative power and energy into our world.

3. BOUNTY: SUMMER

Pour the third cup: This cup is light red (red with white) wine or juice.

Serve the third fruit: This fruit should be soft throughout (strawberry, fig, raisin, grape.)

Make a blessing over the wine—the *kiddush*:

בָּרוּךְ אַתָּה יהוה אֱלֹהֵינוּ מֶלֶךְ הָעוֹלָם בּוֹרֵא פְּרִי הַגָּפֶן׃

Baruḥ atah adonay eloheynu meleḥ ha'olam borey peri hagafen.
Blessed are You, Holy One, life of all worlds, who creates the fruit of the vine.

Make a blessing over the fruit of the earth:

בָּרוּךְ אַתָּה יהוה אֱלֹהֵינוּ מֶלֶךְ הָעוֹלָם בּוֹרֵא פְּרִי הָאֲדָמָה׃

Baruḥ atah adonay eloheynu meleḥ ha'olam borey peri ha'adamah.
Blessed are You, Holy One, life of all worlds, who creates the fruit of the earth.

Reading:
When God created the first human beings,
God led them around the Garden of Eden and said:
Look at my works! See how beautiful they are—how excellent!
I created them all for your sake.
See to it that you do not spoil and destroy my world—for if you do, there
will be no one else to repair it.
—*Midrash Ecclesiastes Rabba (c. 800 CE)*

Green pledge:

— BECAUSE our planet today faces severe environmental crises such as
global warming, rainforest devastation, rapidly increasing popula-
tion, and water and air pollution...

— BECAUSE the planet's future depends on the commitment of every
nation, as well as every individual...

I pledge to do my share in saving and protecting the planet by letting my
concern for the environment shape how I act, purchase, and vote.

4. THANKFULNESS: AUTUMN

Pour the fourth cup: This cup is red wine or juice.

Serve the fourth fruit: This fruit should be chocolate.

Make a blessing over the wine—the *kiddush*:

בָּרוּךְ אַתָּה יהוה אֱלֹהֵינוּ מֶלֶךְ הָעוֹלָם בּוֹרֵא פְּרִי הַגָּפֶן:

Baruḥ atah adonay eloheynu meleḥ ha'olam borey peri hagafen.
Blessed are You, Holy One, life of all worlds, who creates the fruit of the vine.

REPAIR THE WORLD: TZEDAKAH OPPORTUNITY

*Tu Bishvat celebrates our connection to the natural world and our responsibility
to respond to environmental needs. One way to celebrate the New Year of the
Trees is to remember that it's up to you (along with your family and your friends)
to actively work to preserve the world. One national Jewish organization that
responds: A Jewish Response to the Environmental Crisis, www.coejl.org.*

Make a blessing over the fruit of the earth:

בָּרוּךְ אַתָּה יהוה אֱלֹהֵינוּ מֶלֶךְ הָעוֹלָם בּוֹרֵא פְּרִי הָאֲדָמָה:

Baruḥ atah adonay eloheynu meleḥ ha'olam borey peri ha'adamah.
Blessed are You, Holy One, life of all worlds, who creates the fruit of the earth.

Share this story:

Once a man named Honi was walking down the road. He saw an old woman planting trees. "Why are you planting trees, old woman? When they are big and strong enough to produce shade for you and fruit for you, you will no longer be alive."

The old woman answered, "I am planting trees because when I was a baby, my parents planted trees for me. I plant for the sake of my children and grandchildren."

It says in the Talmud, "A person's life is sustained by trees. Just as others have planted for you, plant for the sake of your children."

Sing the *Oseh Shalom*: *Oseh shalom bimromav, hu ya'aseh shalom aleinu, v'al kol yisrael v'imru, v'imru amen. Ya'aseh shalom, ya'aseh shalom, shalom aleinu v'al kol yisrael, ya'aseh shalom, ya'aseh shalom, shalom aleinu v'al kol yisrael.*
May the Holy One, who makes peace in high places, make peace for us and for all Israel, and let us say Amen.

SUGGESTED TU BISHVAT MENU

Good at a "tree planting" picnic.
Pumpernickel bread
Bean barley soup
Fresh apples
Oatmeal chocolate chip cookies

New Rituals

Ways to Make Tu Bishvat *Your Own*

Tu Bishvat Tzedakah **Practice**

Tu Bishvat is a time to tax the fruit of your Tree, the Tree of (your) Life. On the evening of *Tu Bishvat*, go outside into the "soul light" of the full moon. Bring with you three fruits—one with a shell, one with a pit, and one that is edible all the way through—a *tzedakah* box, and lots of quarters. The fruits represent the harvest of your Tree and the *tzedakah* box is for the tax.

Starting with the shelled fruit and finishing with the one that is edible all the way through, hold the fruit close to your heart, ask the questions suggested, and simply receive whatever insight that comes to you. Then say a blessing and eat the fruit.

1. Shelled fruit (orange, coconut): Ask God to reveal to you where you are harvesting hardness when what you need is softness. Where do you need to be vulnerable but end up being defensive?

When you are ready, put some quarters in your *tzedakah* box, saying: "This is to redeem me from unnecessary harshness and defensiveness. With this tax, I pay my debt and move on."

Make a blessing over the fruit of the earth:

בָּרוּךְ אַתָּה יהוה אֱלֹהֵינוּ מֶלֶךְ הָעוֹלָם בּוֹרֵא פְּרִי הָאֲדָמָה:

Baruḫ atah adonay eloheynu meleḫ ha'olam borey peri ha'adamah.
Blessed are You, Holy One, life of all worlds, who creates the fruit of the earth.

2. Pitted fruit (peach, olive, plum, date): Ask God to reveal to you where you are harvesting softness when what you need are boundaries. Where do you need to say "no" but end up saying "yes" instead?

When you are ready, put some quarters in your *tzedakah* box, saying: "This is to redeem me from unnecessary yielding. With this tax, I pay my debt and move on."

Make a blessing over the fruit of the earth:

בָּרוּךְ אַתָּה יהוה אֱלֹהֵינוּ מֶלֶךְ הָעוֹלָם בּוֹרֵא פְּרִי הָאֲדָמָה:

Baruh atah adonay eloheynu meleh ha'olam borey peri ha'adamah.
Blessed are You, Holy One, life of all worlds, who creates the fruit of the earth.

3. Edible all the way through (grape, fig): Ask God to reveal to you where you are harvesting absolute vulnerability and total surrender. Where are you totally resting in a good part of your life? When are you at peace?

When you are ready, put some quarters in your *tzedakah* box, saying: "This is to give thanks for the gift of surrender. With this gift, I honor that gift."

Make a blessing over the fruit of the earth:

בָּרוּךְ אַתָּה יהוה אֱלֹהֵינוּ מֶלֶךְ הָעוֹלָם בּוֹרֵא פְּרִי הָאֲדָמָה:

Baruh atah adonay eloheynu meleh ha'olam borey peri ha'adamah.
Blessed are You, Holy One, life of all worlds, who creates the fruit of the earth.

So now what do you do with the money in your *tzedakah* box? Plant trees. If there is enough money, plant a tree in Israel (www.jnf.org) and/or a tree in your hometown (www.releaf.org), and purchase a plant for your home to remind you of your ongoing promises in this New Year of the Trees.

GARDENING FOR THE SOUL: PLANT TREES

Tu Bishvat calls you to plant trees. Maybe you can still do this in your area. Perhaps you can donate money to plant trees in Israel, or in support of local greening efforts. The first trees to bloom each year in Israel arethe flowering almond trees. Trees help us put life in perspective.

PERSONAL REFLECTIONS

Take a few moments to jot down ideas or things you've experimented with to make this holiday meaningful for you: recipes, something someone said that touched you, a promise or hope that you want to journal about....

Blessing

Blessing for Tu Bishvat

During the coming week
May you enjoy good health and happiness.

May peace reign over our country
And throughout the world.

May you feel your connection to the Tree of Life
Knowing you stand firmly planted on this earth.

May you always have
Something beautiful to look at
Even if it is only a flower in a jelly jar.

May you see potential in a pine cone
And see the future in a peach pit.

And may you plant a carob tree, or an olive tree,
Knowing that you plant for your grandchildren
To enjoy the shade and the fruit.

May the spirit of *Tu Bishvat* enter your heart and connect you to all creation
And may you meet your beloved on the streets of Jerusalem
In the year to come.

Amen.

Like the days of a tree, shall be the days of my people
—Isaiah 65:22

And from the ground the Holy One caused to grow every
tree that was pleasing to the sight and good or food, and
the Tree of Life was in the middle of the garden
—Genesis 2:9

She is a Tree of Life to those who hold fast to her,
she is the Lady, the Shehinah
—Zohar

When a fruit bearing tree is cut down,
its cry carries from one end of the world to the other,
but we cannot hear the sound
—Midrash

Live harmoniously upon the earth,
in peace and with assurance
—Psalm 37

chapter EIGHT

PURIM: MASKING AND UNMASKING

"Purim (Adar) is the month of laughter."
—*Midrash*

Personal Moment

Reverse Halloween—and Thank You, Miss Magarus

Inspired by the gift-giving holiday spirit of *Purim* celebrations in Israel, one year I decided to send *shela̱h manot* (a *Purim* gift) to all our friends within walking distance. With the somewhat reluctant help of my kids (four- and six-year-olds are much more interested in receiving gifts than in giving them), I set up an assembly-line production system on our dining room table. Each plate was quickly filled with two of everything—home-baked *hamantaschen*, little jars of gourmet delicacies, chocolates, and fruits. We wrapped the plates in colored cellophane secured with ribbons and streamers.

"It's sort of a reverse Halloween," I explained to the kids, as we began gifting our neighbors with *Purim* treats. They got into it, and we were all having a good time until our holiday parade took us to Miss Magarus's house. "We're not going there," my kids adamantly protested. "She's mean. We don't even go on Halloween—she never answers the door! She's too scary."

Somehow, I convinced them to go up to the door while I remained on the driveway. After much ringing and knocking, the door opened slowly, revealing a small, gray-haired wisp of a woman who looked at the gift plate in wonder. She invited us in, and it quickly became clear that she was very hard of hearing and very lonely. She gave us juice and tea, and told us stories of what the neighborhood was like when she was a young girl.

When we left, we all agreed that we had received a very special *Purim* gift of our own.

CREATE YOUR OWN MEMORIES

Use this space to jot down Purim *childhood memories or something that happened this year that you want to remember—maybe a precious photo belongs here.*

Meditation

A Meditation for Purim

Sit in a quiet, comfortable place. You'll need a hand mirror that's large enough so that when you look into it, you can see your entire face. Place the mirror face down and settle into a quiet comfort.

Purim is a time of hiddenness and a time of revelation. Esther's name even means "hidden" in Hebrew.

Think of the hidden essence of yourself. Name the qualities that describe your true self, the things you admire about yourself, the best parts of who you are.

Look into the mirror with loving awareness.

See those hidden best qualities in your eyes, around your mouth, in your smile.

On *Purim*, people wear masks to hide their identities.

Look into the mirror for the hidden spark of the divine that is in you. Relax into acceptance of who you are.

Your hidden self is a joyful self. Smile at yourself in the mirror.

Think of a joyful recent moment. Watch your face soften into a smile of connection with that good memory.

Reveal the joy hidden inside you.

Infuse yourself with happiness.

Uncover the love you have for people and for God's world.

Imagine the world joyful and happy.

SPIRITUAL CHOCOLATE MOMENT

Take a private moment to enjoy a chocolate dessert this Purim. Purim *is all about joy—you deserve a joyful chocolate moment. Lori Longbotham in* Luscious Chocolate Desserts *promises: "After a good hot fudge sundae you may feel like you've sighed and gone to heaven."*

Story

A Purim Story

Pinhas was the poorest disciple of his teacher, the great Maggid of Poland. On *Purim*, it was the custom in this community to line up and present a gift to the great Maggid and receive a blessing.

Poor Pinhas, stooped over and looking at the floor, stood in line with everyone else to greet the shining light of that generation, the great Maggid. When it was finally his turn, he greeted his rabbi in a soft, almost expressionless voice. "Good *Purim*." He was ready to leave right away because he was embarrassed that he had no gift for his *rebbe*.

The *rebbe* said to him, "Pinhas, why didn't you bring me a gift for *Purim*?"

Pinhas replied, "I have a wife and seven children. We have nothing to eat. I do not have money to buy you *shelah manot* [a *Purim* gift]."

"Pinhas, you know what your problem is? You don't know how to say 'Good *Purim*.'"

The rebbe then demonstrated how one should say "Good *Purim*." He yelled, "*GOOD PURIM! GOOD PURIM*, PINHAS!"

He told Pinhas to stand up tall, as tall as he could, and yell back to him, "GOOD *PURIM*!"

They yelled "GOOD *PURIM*!" to each other several times. Pinhas started to feel better and better.

Finally, the rebbe told him, "Pinhas, go out and get me *shelah manot*."

Pinhas left and went to the one neighborhood grocery store in the town. In the past, Pinhas would usually stand by the door of the store on Friday before *Shabbat*, and people would give him various foods as they left the store. From this his family would live from week to week.

But on this *Purim*, he actually walked right into the store. "Good *Purim*! Good *Purim*!" he cried. "Give me the biggest cake and the finest bottle of wine. I have to bring *shelah manot* to my *rebbe*. I'll pay you tomorrow."

If he had said this before, he would have been thrown out of the store. But now, the owner brought him the cake and wine he requested. Pinhas returned to the Holy Maggid, and as soon as he approached the *rebbe*, he yelled to him, "Good *Purim*, Holy Maggid!" And the *rebbe* yelled back, "Good *Purim*, Pinhas!"

Pinhas gave the *Purim* gift to the *rebbe*.

The *rebbe* then said, "I want to give you *shelah manot* back. I am giving you the gift that *Purim* should be with you all year long. The strength of *Purim* should be with you forever."

Pinhas walked away a new person. He went back to the grocery store and said again to the owner, "Good *Purim*. My family has nothing to eat. Give me some food and I'll pay you tomorrow." The owner brought out the most extraordinary box of delicacies.

Pinhas went to a clothing store and said, "Good *Purim*, I need clothes for my children. I'll pay you after *Purim*." And they gave him beautiful clothes for his seven children. He passed by a women's boutique. He thought of his wife, reflecting on how beautiful she used to be. He entered the store. "Good *Purim*! Please give me some nice dresses for my wife. I'll pay you tomorrow." And soon he had bags of beautiful dresses.

A Bissel (Little) Yiddish

Hamantasch is a Yiddish word meaning "Haman's pocket" and refers to the tri-corner cookie stuffed with fruit, poppy seeds, or chocolate. It is said to derive from bribes stuffing this corrupt villain's pockets. Hamantasch is the plural form. In Hebrew: "oznay Haman" (Haman's ears)

He went home and yelled, "Good *Purim*! Good *Purim*!" to his children and his wife. He looked them straight in the eye and said, "I have not been a good father or husband, but now I promise I will be *better*. The Holy *rebbe* blessed me with the strength of *Purim*. Everything will change now. The first thing I want to do is teach you to say 'Good *Purim*.'"

He told his children to stand up straight, and he yelled, "Good *Purim*, wonderful children!" And the children yelled back, "Good *Purim*!" He yelled to his wife, "Good *Purim*, beautiful wife!" She yelled back to him, "Good *Purim*!" They did this several times. There soon grew a feeling of love, blessing, and abundance in their home.

After *Purim*, the newly confident Pin<u>h</u>as went to the richest Jew in town and said to him, "The Holy Maggid blessed me with the strength of *Purim*. Would you lend me 10,000 rubles? I will pay it back to you in four weeks." And with this loan he started a business, and he soon became the richest Jew in Poland. And he provided for his family and the poor of his community for the rest of his life.

Reflections

Purim *Reflections*

Purim calls us to give free rein to be joyous and foolish, silly and uninhibited. For the sake of Torah and ourselves, we need *Purim* to laugh at what we value and thus paradoxically gain a real sense of self-worth.

In the Bible we read:

"They were to observe them as days of feasting and merrymaking, and as an occasion for sending gifts to one another and presents to the poor."
—*Esther, 9:22*

"They were to observe them as days of feasting…"
Purim is unique because it celebrates a salvation that does not come from God alone. Recorded in the Book of Esther, human actors have center stage. We bring about our own redemption.

Purim commemorates the deliverance, some 2,500 years ago, of the Jews of the Persian Empire from the total annihilation plotted by Haman, the prime minister at the court of King Ahasuerus. This last-minute rescue was brought about by the intercession of beautiful Queen Esther and by the steadfast faith of her cousin Mordecai, a decent Jew well-known and esteemed in court circles. In the end, Haman was hanged, and Mordecai succeeded to this high post.

"...and merrymaking..."
The festival of *Purim* is a grand farce, filled with coincidence and the absurdities of luck where the right person is always in the right place at the right time (Esther and Mordecai) or in the wrong place at the wrong time (Haman).

The Book of Esther, read from a scroll similar to the Torah scroll, is called a *megillah*. The story is very unlike anything in the five books of the Torah: In the book of Esther, the hero is a woman and God's name is never mentioned.

To face one another and ourselves as we are—this is the work of *Purim*. *Purim* is a time to let ourselves be more open and generous with each other, to be more aware of our own opportunities to make the world a better place.

"...as an occasion for sending gifts to one another..."
A custom of generosity is observed, *mishloah manot* (sending gifts of food to friends and relatives), because *Purim* is a time of love and friendship.

"...and presents to the poor."
Mattanot le-evyonim (presents to the poor) is the special custom of giving *tzedakah* money to two poor people or charities. A related custom is called *mahazit ha-shekel* (half of a *shekel* coin). In ancient Israel, each person owed half a *shekel* for the upkeep of the Temple. This tax was collected around the time of *Purim*. Over time, this custom has become an additional opportunity to give to the poor. Some give silver dollars, recalling the appearance of the *shekel*. Some people start a new *tzedakah* box at *Purim* and try to fill it up by *Passover*.

May this *Purim* fill us with a sense of generosity and the ability to see ourselves and others as created in the image of God. May we celebrate this *Purim* with gifts of the heart, gratitude for the blessings in our own lives, and generosity toward others. At *Purim* we recognize that redemption, making the world a better place, is up to us. At *Purim* we need to forge our own redemption as the Jews in the Book of Esther do. *Purim* is a joyous holiday, a holiday created by humans, reflecting human endeavors. There are no miracles in the Book of Esther. Creating miracles in our world is up to us!

Celebration of Tradition

What to Do to Celebrate Purim

Perform the four main mitzvot of *Purim*: We remember them because they all begin with the letter "M."

Megillat Esther: Read the story of *Purim* in the evening and the next day. Whenever Haman is mentioned, make as much noise as possible to drown out his name and his memory!

Mishloa*<u>*h*</u>*Manot: Send gifts of food to at least one friend or relative, because *Purim* is a time of love and friendship among Jews.

Matanot L'Evyoneem: Give gifts of money and/or food to the poor, because *Purim* is a time of sharing, caring, and helping.

Mishteh: Eat a festive *Purim* meal. This special holiday meal should be eaten on *Purim* afternoon.

SUGGESTED PURIM MENU

Make **shala**<u>**h**</u> **manot** *(gift baskets) for family and friends.*
Hamantaschen
Zucchini bread
Dried fruit
Pomegranate (or another exotic) fruit juice or wine

New Rituals

Ways to Make Purim *Your Own*

Make a *Purim* flag: A new *Purim* ritual invites us to make a flag with Vashti and Esther on it and wave the flag when their names are mentioned during the megillah reading. Currently, the rituals and symbols associated with *Purim* do not evoke either Esther or Vashti. At least symbolically, the fact that the grager and its noise are the prominent symbols and sounds of *Purim* serve to put Haman, hatred, and celebrating violent retribution at the center of communal celebrations of *Purim*.

In contrast, the primary purpose of the *Purim* flag is to call attention to Esther and Vashti and make it fun to listen for their names. But the *Purim* flag offers us an opportunity to do more than balance our attention to men's names with attention to women's names. When we wave our flags at the mention of Vashti and Esther's names, we begin to shift the focus of *Purim*. No longer do we need to accept that the opposition of "blessed Mordecai" and "cursed Haman" is the whole story of *Purim* or the story of Jewish experience. By focusing on Vashti and Esther **as well as** Haman and Mordecai, we open up the possibility of telling a more complete and complex *Purim* story, a story that includes the experiences of women and a story that honors the possibility of potential alliances between Jews and non-Jews.

GARDENING FOR THE SOUL: FRUIT TREES

Planting fruit trees gives you a real sense of achievement. If you have a plum tree in your garden, honor it by using plum preserves to stuff inside your **hamantaschen.** *You might place a nameplate near your fruit trees that says "I'm a Purim* Plum Tree." *You can use any fruit preserves in baking* **Purim** *treats.*

Personal Reflections

Take a few moments to jot down ideas or things you've experimented with to make this holiday meaningful for you: recipes, something someone said that touched you, a promise or hope that you want to journal about....

Blessing

A Blessing for Purim

On *Purim* we wear masks and hide,
as Esther masked her true identity.
But we put them on only to better take them off.
So accustomed are we to wearing of masks
that we forget the One that supports them.
But mask-wearing is our norm, not our problem;
it is mask-removing that is the true challenge of *Purim*.

To remove our masks,
to face one another and ourselves as we are:
images on the digital screen of the universe—
this is the work of *Purim*.

May this *Purim* find you with the courage
to remove the mask
and perceive the One.
May this *Purim* find you ready to look
beyond diversity
to the mirrored unity reflected in each and every soul.

Amen.

REPAIR THE WORLD: TZEDAKAH OPPORTUNITY

On Purim, we give gifts to our friends and to the poor and needy in our community. This holiday invites you (along with friends and family) to visit the sick and needy in your neighborhood and bring them something as simple as a plate of cookies. The real gift is the gift of your time and attention, letting others know that you care about them. One national Jewish organization that responds: the National Center for Jewish Healing www.ncjh.org.

When we enter Adar we increase in joy
—Talmud

The month was transformed from one of grief to one of joy
—Esther 9:22

As the morning star breaks through at dawn,
so is the redemption brought by Esther to Israel
—Midrash

chapter NINE

PASSOVER: FACING FREEDOM

"Every one of us must see ourselves as if I went out of Egypt"
—*Talmud*

Personal Moment

Celebrating Miriam

At the heart of our synagogue's Women's *Seder* lives the spirit of Miriam, the prophetess. Miriam, who took her tambourine in hand and led us in celebration after crossing the Red Sea. Miriam, who inspires hope and confidence, who still leads us by her example of courage and wisdom.

At a recent *Seder*, we were invited to celebrate the "Miriams" in our own life—the mothers and *bubbes*, the *tantes* and teachers, the sisters and mentors. We began our celebration by writing words of blessing, prayer, or dedication to our "Miriams." We gathered at tables in the foyer, chose a colored ribbon, grabbed a marker, and opened up our hearts.

Here is what some of our participants wrote:

"To all of the mothers who went before me with love, strength, and devotion to their family..."

"To all the strong, compassionate, jubilant, honest, caring women who rock the world."

"Grandma Edna, you taught me to speak my mind and have money in my own name! You loved me so much..."

"For Rose and Sylvia, who shaped and dressed me. For Miriam and her well-lived life. For Peppy. Always present in my thoughts."

Each completed ribbon was attached by Velcro to an enormous tambourine. The completed tambourines floated above the *Seder* tables, crowned with ribbons of purple, gold, rose, and orange that were filled with deep personal meaning, filled with life.

CREATE YOUR OWN MEMORIES

Use this space to jot down Passover childhood memories or something that happened this year that you want to remember—maybe a precious photo belongs here.

Meditation

A Meditation for Passover

Sit in a relaxed, easy pose. You'll need pen, paper, matches, and a small bowl of water.

Bring your attention to your feet, your shins, your knees, allowing each part of your body to relax as you bring your attention there. Finish with the back of your neck and the crown of your head, feeling an easing of tension.

Passover is the time of personal liberation. The Hebrew word for Egypt is *mitzrayim*, or "narrow straits."

Think of something you wish to free yourself of: a habit, an addiction, a negative relationship, a destructive thought that keeps running through your head.

Take a small piece of paper and write down what is trapping you in "narrow straits"—in your personal Egypt.

Take a match and burn the strip of paper and drop it in a small bowl of water nearby.

Celebrate the moment of freedom. Know that you have liberated yourself. Even if only for the moment, you have come out of Egypt.

Promise to liberate yourself as often as you need to from whatever is keeping you enslaved. Celebrate your moments of triumph.

Allow freedom to become a habit.

Story

An Iraqi Folktale

Many years ago in Baghdad, there lived a good couple who loved God, gave *tzedakah*, and helped the poor. All of Baghdad honored the couple, and yet they had one sorrow: They had no children. Years passed, and one day, as the couple sat at their *Passover Seder* table, they read the *Haggadah* and retold the Exodus. Yet the wife was sad, as she always was at *Passover*. Her husband understood the reason for her grief and comforted her as he always did: "Don't worry, we'll have a child one day. God won't forget us."

While the husband and wife were talking, there was a sudden knock at the door. At the threshold stood a ragged old man. The couple invited him to join their *Seder* and treated him with the greatest hospitality. However, when the old man took his leave of the pair who had hosted him so kindly, he turned to them, and instead of thanking them, said, "I pray to God that next year your *Pesaḥ* table will be a wreck!" The ungrateful old man's curse astonished the couple and angered them, but out of respect, they said nothing. A month later, the wife discovered that she was pregnant! And indeed, two months before the next *Passover*, a son was finally born to them. Their great joy could not be described, and the old man and his curse were, of course, forgotten.

The next *Passover*, the couple sat around the *Seder* table and read the *Haggadah* with their son. The baby behaved like all babies do. He laughed and fussed and tipped over the wine. He knocked over the cups and broke the plates. But his mother and father loved their only child so much that they took pleasure even in the havoc he wreaked. This was the son they had prayed for year after year. It was only at the end of the *Seder* that the couple remembered the old man and his "curse" that their *Pesaḥ* table would be a wreck! This was indeed a blessing in disguise, and the old man, they had no doubt in their hearts, was none other than Elijah himself.

SPIRITUAL CHOCOLATE MOMENT

Judith Viorst defines strength as "the capacity to break a chocolate bar into four pieces with your bare hands—and then eat just one of the pieces." **Passover** *chocolate can be very good. Celebrate freedom from dietary vigilance and enjoy!*

Reflection

Perhaps the most widely celebrated of all Jewish holidays, *Passover* celebrates the Exodus from Egypt, a moment of liberation, a clean slate, a new beginning.

Passover Reflections

In the Torah we read:

"You shall observe the Feast of Unleavened Bread as an institution for all time."
—*Exodus 12:17*

and

"You shall explain to your child on that day, it is because of what the Holy One did for me when I went free from Egypt."
—*Exodus 13:8*

"You shall observe the Feast of Unleavened Bread..."
All leavening agents are known as *ḥametz*. As we engage in the removal of *ḥametz* from our homes in preparation for *Passover* (for *matzot*, our unleavened bread), we engage in a profoundly personal experience as well. On a symbolic level, *ḥametz* represents unnecessary suffering and pain that enslave us to bitterness. The idea at *Passover* is to destroy *ḥametz*—physical, emotional, and spiritual *ḥametz*. We are cleaning our homes and cleaning our hearts. As we search our darkened homes for the last bits of *ḥametz*, we search inside ourselves and try to get rid of our own sources of internal corruption and fermented anger.

"...as an institution for all time."
From the *Haggadah* we read, "In every generation, each individual should feel personally redeemed from Egypt." This is not only the heart of the *Seder* and of the celebration of *Passover*, but the heart of Judaism as well. We are to find our own story within the mythic story of liberation and recommit to it every year. The message of hope at the core—that it is possible to transform our lives and heal our broken world—is the gift of the Jewish people to the world for all time.

...continued on page156

A Bissel (Little) Yiddish

*During the week of **Passover**, say "GUT MOYED" (Happy In-Between Times).*
In Hebrew: "Moadim l'simḥa" (Happy Times).

PERSONAL REFLECTIONS

Take a few moments to jot down ideas or things you've experimented with to
make this holiday meaningful for you: recipes, something someone said that touched you,
a promise or hope that you want to journal about....

"You shall explain to your child on that day..."
In the Talmud we learn "God created us because the Holy One loves stories." *Passover* is the opportunity to tell our stories to our children and to each other. We share not only the great story of the Exodus, but our own personal moments of triumph over despair and redemption from terrible situations and experiences. By weaving our own stories into the master story, we renew the fabric of our lives, strengthen our families, and deepen our relationships.

"...it is because of what the Holy One did for me when I went free from Egypt."
To be free from Egypt means to be free from "narrow straits" because that is what the Hebrew word for Egypt, *mitzrayim*, means. We celebrate freedom from political and religious repression. We commit to helping those in the world who are not yet free. We honor and commit ourselves to freedom from slavery on all levels and in all places. As we appreciate what it means to be free from external oppression and our own inner oppression, we remind ourselves of the responsibilities that come with the gift of freedom.

Celebration of Tradition

What to Do to Celebrate Passover

Prepare the *Seder* plate: The *Seder* plate contains all the symbols of the *Seder*. While any dish can be used, many people own special *Seder* plates with places marked for each item. One *Seder* plate is enough, though some people provide more if the *Seder* is very large. The items on the *Seder* plate include:

Karpas—a vegetable, usually green such as parsley, symbolizing spring and rebirth. It is dipped in salt water near the beginning of the *Seder*.

Haroset—a mixture of chopped apples, nuts, wine or grape juice, and spices. The haroset symbolizes the mortar that the slaves made for bricks in Egypt and is used to offset the taste of the bitter herbs. Recipes vary widely among Jews, though the above list of ingredients is the most common among Ashkenazi Jews. Sephardic recipes often include figs, dates, raisins, and bananas as well.

Maror—the bitter herbs. Either romaine lettuce or freshly ground or sliced horseradish is used as a symbol of the bitterness of slavery.

Beytzah—roasted egg, symbol of the festival sacrifice. The egg should be hard-boiled and then, still in its shell, placed on a stove burner or in the oven until part of it is scorched.

Zeroa—roasted shank bone, symbol of the *Pesah* sacrifice. The rabbis of the Talmud also allow a broiled beet, which is helpful for vegetarians.

Hazeret—additional *maror* to be used for Hillel's sandwich. Some *Seder* plates include this sixth symbol.

Orange—the orange represents the full and equal role of women in Judaism and is a symbol of honoring the marginalized and disenfranchised people in our world. Here's the story: Dr. Susanna Heschel, daughter of the great liberal rabbi Abraham Joshua Heschel, heard a prominent rabbi dismiss the changing roles of women (and others marginalized in the 20th century) by comparing them to placing an orange on the *Seder* plate. She suggested we do exactly that! Incorporate an orange on your *Seder* plate to represent the inclusion of the marginalized and as a validation of women's central place and equal rights in Jewish life. She called it a "juicy validation."

...continued on page 160

SUGGESTED PASSOVER MENU

Gefilte fish

Chicken soup with matzah balls

Rosemary roast chicken

Carrot ring

Asparagus

Fresh fruit

Macaroons

OR

Tossed salad

Spinach cheese bake

Layered vegetable terrine

Frozen strawberry meringue torte

Prepare the *Seder* table: Other items are integral to the celebration of the holiday. These include:

Matzot—Three *matzot*, placed one atop the other, are used during the *Seder*. They are customarily covered with a napkin or *matzah* cover and placed next to the *Seder* plate. Use plain flour and water *matzah* for the *Seder*, symbolizing *leḥem oni*—the plain bread of affliction.

Wine or grape juice—Four cups of wine or grape juice are drunk during the course of the *Seder*. The drinking of the four cups is a *mitzvah*, not an endurance test. Since it's important to be fully conscious at the *Seder* rather than sleepy or tipsy, you can alternate wine and juice, or use only juice. If, for health reasons, you cannot drink grape juice or wine, any other drink can be used.

Salt water—Bowls of salt water are placed on the table as a symbol of the tears of slavery. The *karpas*, or green vegetable, is dipped into the salt water early in the *Seder*.

Miriam's Cup and Elijah's Cup—A large goblet is set in the center of the table at the beginning of the *Seder*, symbolizing the well of Miriam that sustained the Israelites during their journey in the desert. It should be filled with spring water. A large goblet, filled with wine, is set aside for Elijah, who represents the longing for perfection at the end of time, which, according to legend, will be heralded by Elijah. Some legends hold that the prophet visits every home on *Pesaḥ* and drinks from his cup.

Pillows—People use pillows to lean on whenever we are called upon to recline during the *Seder*. The custom of reclining goes back to ancient times, when slaves ate standing up while free people ate while reclining.

The order of the *Seder*:
Kadesh—blessing over wine or grape juice
Urḥatz—hand-washing
Karpas—dipping a vegetable in salt water
Yaḥatz—breaking the middle *matzah*
Magid—telling the story
Raḥtzah—hand-washing
Motzi matzah—eating *matzah*
Maror—eating bitter herbs
Koreḥ—eating *matzah* and *maror* sandwich
Shulḥan oreḥ—the meal
Tzafun—eating the *afikomen*
Bareḥ—blessings after the meal
Hallel—reciting Psalms
Nirtzaḥ—the conclusion

Ways to Make Passover Your Own

Search for _hametz_ (the last crumbs): During the week prior to _Pesah_, we clean our houses to remove all _hametz_ (leaven—i.e., bread or cookie crumbs) from our possession. On the night before the _Pesah Seder_, a symbolic search for _hametz_ is conducted using a feather, a candle, and a wooden spoon. We "find" a few bread crumbs that have been hidden especially for this ritual and use the feather to coax them onto a wooden spoon. A candle is lit and the bread crumbs are burned. When the crumbs are consumed by the fire, we are free of _hametz_ and ready to prepare for the _Seder_. As we engage in the removal of _hametz_ from our homes, we engage in a profoundly personal experience as well. On a symbolic level, _hametz_ represents any corrupting or fermenting feelings or stories we hold onto until we find ourselves enslaved by bitterness. The idea at _Pesah_ is to destroy _hametz_—physical, emotional, and spiritual _hametz_. As we search our darkened homes for the last bits of _hametz_, we search our hearts as well.

Take a few moments now to ask yourselves:
- What is enslaving me to bitterness?
- What do I need to escape from, internally and externally?
- What must I do to be free?

Explore the notion of eco-_hametz_: _Hasidic_ teachers saw _hametz_ metaphorically as the swelling up of excess in our own lives. In this sense, is overconsumption _hametz_? And is _Passover_ teaching us to simplify our lives? Who or what is Pharaoh in our world today, bringing eco-disastrous plagues upon our heads? What must we do? This offers good discussion at your _Seder_ table.

GARDENING FOR THE SOUL: PLANTING GRASS

On the second day of **Passover**, in ancient Israel, an early crop of barley was planted. Plant some easily grown ornamental grasses in a pretty container and notice how quickly they grow during the seven weeks between **Passover** and **Shavuot**. Celebrate the simple beauty of tender growing grass. Because this is almost foolproof, this is great to do with kids.

Fill Miriam's Cup: At the *Seder*, some place a "Cup of Miriam" (filled with water) beside the customary "Cup of Elijah" (filled with wine). The cup contains water in memory of Miriam's well, which, according to a *Midrash* (an interpretive legend), accompanied the Israelites on their journey through the desert. I like to use an empty cup for Miriam. Pass the cup around the table, inviting each person to share a *Passover* hope or memory as they pour a little bit of water from their own water glass into Miriam's Cup. Miriam's Cup becomes filled with water and with our memories, stories and hopes.

Reclaim the *Haggadah*:
1. There is no mitzvah to starve! Not by parsley alone shall we survive.
2. You don't have to read the whole *Haggadah*, just tell stories.
3. Decrease cleaning and cooking; increase planning a participatory *Seder*.
4. Make the Exodus contemporary—politically and personally.
5. Make the *Seder* fun, "for only the lesson enjoyed is the lesson learned"

—*Rabbi Yehuda Hanasi, third century*

Personal Reflections

Take a few moments to jot down ideas or things you've experimented with to make this holiday meaningful for you: recipes, something someone said that touched you, a promise or hope that you want to journal about....

Blessing

A Blessing for Passover

During the coming week
May you enjoy good health and happiness.

May peace reign over our country
And throughout the world.

May this be a joyous and sweet *Pesaḥ*
for you and those you love.

May you remember the miraculous
in your own life this *Passover*.

May you pass through narrow
and difficult places in your life.

When you eat *matzah*, the bread of affliction,
May you take a bite out of that which afflicts you.

May you chew away at it, layer by layer
Until you clear a channel
for your soul to feel open and free.

May you always walk purposefully through life
As we did at the parting of the sea,
For movement without direction
Will create a hole in the ground.

May all your *matzah* balls be light.

May Elijah the Prophet enter your house
and grant you peace
And may you meet your beloved
on the streets of Jerusalem in the year to come.

Amen.

I will take you out of the misery of Egypt to a land
flowing with milk and honey
—Exodus 3:17

For that child, you must begin the story
—Passover Haggadah

The winter of slavery is over
—Midrash

Out of Egypt, in the wilderness, they began to flourish
—Midrash

chapter TEN
PASSOVER TO SHAVUOT:
SEVEN WEEKS TO COUNT THE OMER

"A time for every purpose under heaven"
-*Ecclesiastes 3:1*

Counting the *Omer*

Mystical Judaism invites us to commit to seven weeks of practice as a holy and meaningful period of time. Seven weeks contain a sevenfold power, seven weeks of seven days. The seven weeks between *Passover (Pesaḥ)* and the Festival of Weeks *(Shavuot)* are an especially meaningful time to do personal spiritual work. This is known as the period of "Counting the *Omer*." Between *Passover* and *Shavuot* we count off 49 days (seven weeks plus one more day) of spiritual preparation for the receiving of the Torah on *Shavuot*. During this period, called the *Omer* ("sheaf offering"), we focus internally as we allow ourselves to parallel the story of our people wandering in the desert. Their journey becomes our spiritual journey.

Each of the seven weeks is characterized by one of the mystical attributes of God, and by extension, each of these attributes lives inside us as a divine spark, reminding us that we are created in God's image. Mystical Judaism explains that God's goodness is revealed to and experienced by us through these seven sacred values, which are the character traits of God's own essence. Known in Kabbalah as the lower seven *sefirot* (divine attributes), these seven traits of the divine Self are deeply and intimately embedded within us at birth as soul traits; they exist inside us as the source of our own best selves.

According to this practice, as we count each day of each week, we have the opportunity to focus on a particular quality beginning with *ḥesed* (kindness). Throughout this first week, we work on developing and deepening our own quality of *ḥesed*. The second week is devoted to *gevurah* (restraint), the third week centers on *tiferet* (compassion), the fourth is *netzaḥ* (persistence), the fifth is *hod* (gratitude), then *yesod* (composure), and finally *malḥut* (trust).

As a further refinement in mystical Jewish tradition, each day also has the quality of one of the seven attributes. The personal spiritual work of each day is shown on the *Omer* chart "Counting the *Omer*: 49 Days of Spiritual Growth."

I find it works best for me to focus on each week's attribute. Somehow, I can hold that in my mind as I move through the week. As a daily practice, I try at the beginning of each day, or before I go to sleep the night before, to consider how the unique pairing of attributes of that particular day informs my practice or offers new insights.

Breath Meditation

A practice that helps me work on my character development is breath meditation. Breath meditation takes you on a journey of inner awareness by asking you to focus on breath as your life force, your connection between the physical and spiritual. In meditation you consciously slow down so that you can pay attention to the quieter inner world of your spirit. The breath meditations offered will help you work on your own character development by focusing on verses or phrases from the Book of Psalms and Proverbs.

To practice the following breath meditations, simply focus on the first part of the verse during the in breath and on the second part of the verse with the out breath. It's often helpful to repeat this a few times.

Begin with this prayer.

Blessing for Counting the Omer

Meditate for a moment on the attribute for this week or on the attribute for this day, and say this prayer:

בָּרוּךְ אַתָּה יהוה אֱלֹהֵינוּ מֶלֶךְ הָעוֹלָם, אֲשֶׁר קִדְּשָׁנוּ בְּמִצְוֹתָיו וְצִוָּנוּ עַל סְפִירַת הָעֹמֶר:

Baruh atah adonay, eloheynu meleh ha'olam, asher kideshanu bemitzvotav vetzivanu al sefirat ha-omer.

As I count this day of the *Omer*, may I bring forth, unite, and perfect the qualities of the Holy One as they flow within me. Amen.

(Say the appropriate day and week)

Today is the __ day, which is ___ weeks and ___ days of the *Omer*.

		Hesed *Kindness*	Gevurah *Restraint*	Tiferet *Compassion*
WEEK ONE	Hesed *Kindness*	*Kindness in Kindness* *1*	*Restrain in Kindness* *2*	*Compassion in Kindness*
WEEK TWO	Gevurah *Restraint*	*Kindness in Restraint* *8*	*Restrain in Restraint* *9*	*Compassion in Restraint*
WEEK THREE	Tiferet *Compassion*	*Kindness in Compassion* *15*	*Restrain in Compassion* *16*	*Compassion in Compassion*
WEEK FOUR	Netzah *Persistence*	*Kindness in Persistence* *22*	*Restrain in Persistence* *23*	*Compassion in Persistence*
WEEK FIVE	Hod *Gratitude*	*Kindness in Gratitude* *29*	*Restrain in Gratitude* *30*	*Compassion in Gratitude*
WEEK SIX	Yesod *Composure*	*Kindness in Composure* *36*	*Restrain in Composure* *37*	*Compassion in Composure*
WEEK SEVEN	Malhut *Trust*	*Kindness in Trust* *43*	*Restrain in Trust* *44*	*Compassion in Trust*

9 Days of Spiritual Growth

Netzah Persistence	Hod Gratitude	Yesod Composure	Malhut Trust
Persistence in Kindness 4	Gratitude in Kindness 5	Composure in Kindness 6	Trust in Kindness 7
Persistence in Restraint 11	Gratitude in Restraint 12	Composure in Restraint 13	Trust in Restraint 14
Persistence in Compassion 18	Gratitude in Compassion 19	Composure in Compassion 20	Trust in Compassion 21
Persistence in Persistence 25	Gratitude in Persistence 26	Composure in Persistence 27	Trust in Persistence 28
Persistence in Gratitude 32	Gratitude in Gratitude 33	Composure in Gratitude 34	Trust in Gratitude 35
Persistence in Composure 39	Gratitude in Composure 40	Composure in Composure 41	Trust in Composure 42
Persistence in Trust 46	Gratitude in Trust 47	Composure in Trust 48	Trust in Trust 49

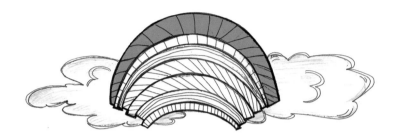

During the first week, days 1–7 on the _Omer_ chart, concentrate on the soul trait of loving kindness. The first century's Rabbi Shimon taught, "The world endures because of loving kindness." The 14th Dalai Lama recently stated, "My true religion is kindness." We exist through a divine act of loving kindness, none of us asked to be born. Now, out of gratitude for the precious gift of life itself, it is up to us to take care of each other. Kindness involves acts and responses that are sustaining to other people, calling us to offer real support to others. Kindness means doing honest and selfless acts motivated by a spirit of generosity.

May these verses inspire your commitment to being a kind and caring person this week.

"The road of loving kindness leads to life." (Proverbs 12:28)
  - In breath: The road of loving kindness
  - Out breath: leads to life.

"Loving kindness is a haven, a refuge in time of trouble." (Psalm 60:17)
  - In breath: Loving kindness is a haven
  - Out breath: a refuge in time of trouble.

"Extend the hand of loving kindness, rescue those who are frightened."
(Psalm 60:7)
  - In breath: Extend the hand of loving kindness
  - Out breath: rescue those who are frightened.

"Send your loving kindness to awaken me and put danger to rest."
(Psalm 57:4)
  - In breath: Send your loving kindness to awaken me
  - Out breath: and put danger to rest.

PERSONAL REFLECTIONS

Use this space to reflect on the importance of loving kindness in your life.

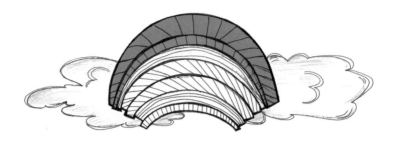

Gevurah invites us to cultivate self-control and restraint. *Gevurah* is often tested when obstacles and difficult situations arise in our lives. Self-discipline is a powerful form of *gevurah*. The practice of *gevurah* builds personal integrity and a sense of responsibility. There is *gevurah* in bringing your awareness to the gift of breath; use it to slow down anger and strengthen restraint.

During the second week, days 8–14 on the *Omer* chart, focus on the soul trait of *Gevurah*—restraint and self-control.

"Create in me a spirit of self-control" (Psalm 51:12)
- In breath: Create in me
- Out breath: a spirit of self-control.

"Dressed in self-control, raging seas are stilled." (Psalm 65:7-8)
- In breath: Dressed in self-control,
- Out breath: raging seas are stilled.

"Follow restraint and become wise." (Proverbs 8:33)
- In breath: Follow restraint
- Out breath: and become wise.

PERSONAL REFLECTIONS

Use this space to reflect on the importance of restraint and self-control in your life.

Third Week: *Tiferet* (Compassion)

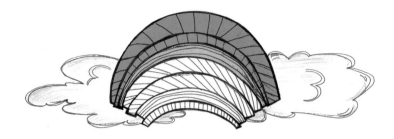

Tiferet is compassionate acceptance, often translated as "beauty" because *tiferet*, which is the heart, perceives the beauty in all things and offers compassion. What kind of person or situation evokes our compassion? Is our compassion tinged with patronizing condescension? Can we be compassionate even with ourselves?

Sit quietly for a few moments as you settle in, noticing your breath and the rise and fall of your chest and belly. Bring your awareness to the miracle of breath, the gift of life itself.

During the third week, days 15–21 on the *Omer* chart, concentrate on the soul trait of compassion.

"Do what is right, that it may go well with you." (Deut 6:18)
- In breath: Do what is right,
- Out breath: that it may go well with you.

"Let me champion the lowly and help the needy." (Psalm 72:4)
- In breath: Let me champion the lowly
- Out breath: and help the needy.

"Let me produce well-being for others." (Psalm 72:3)
- In breath: Let me produce
- Out breath: well-being for others.

PERSONAL REFLECTIONS

Use this space to reflect on moments of compassion in your life.

Yom Ha-Atzma'ut—Israel Independence Day

The 20th day of the counting of the *Omer* is the holiday of Israel Independence Day, *Yom Ha-Atzma'ut*. Israel became independent on May 14, 1948—on the Hebrew calendar, 5 Iyar 5708. In the Torah, *Israel* "means wrestling with God" in Hebrew. In the first book, Genesis, our forefather Jacob, wrestling with a stranger, earned a blessing for his victory: *"Your name shall no longer be Jacob, but Israel, for you have wrestled with beings divine and human and have prevailed." (Genesis 32:29).*

In the spirit of compassion, we celebrate the spirit of the land of Israel, a place of ingathering, a refuge, a home for Jews after many centuries of exile. Israel continues to struggle—with her own problems and with enemies as she searches for compassionate ways to deal with Palestinian Arabs. Today, we join with all of Israel and commit ourselves to finding the way, guided by compassion, toward peace.

Visit Israel: There is nothing else quite like this experience, for yourself and for your family. Israel, as the ancestral home of our people, gives us a sense of rootedness and a bond with the past. Our connection to the land goes back more than 4,000 years.

Eat at an Israeli restaurant: Enjoy pita bread, humus, roast chicken with rosemary, and falafel.

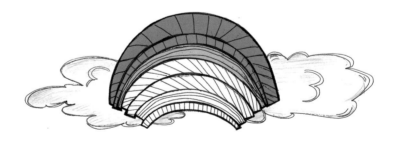

Share a prayer for *Yom Ha'Atzma'ut*:

We pray for Israel,
Both the mystic ideal of our ancestors' dreams,
And the living miracle, here and now,
Built of heart, muscle, and steel.

May she endure and guard her soul,
Surviving the relentless, age-old hatreds,
The cynical concealment of diplomatic deceit,
And the rumblings that warn of war.
May Israel continue to be the temple that magnetizes
The loving eyes of Jews in all corners:

The Jew in a land of affluence and relative peace
Who forgets the glory and pain of his being,
And the Jew in a land of oppression whose bloodied fist
Beats in anguish and pride
Against the cage of his enslavement.

May Israel yet embrace her homeless, her own,
And bind the ingathered into one people.

May those who yearn for a society built on human concern
Find the vision of the prophets realized in her.
May her readiness to defend
Never diminish her search for peace.

May we always dare to hope
That in our day the antagonisms will end,
That all the displaced, Arab and Jew, will be rooted again,
That within Israel and across her borders
All God's children will touch hands in peace.

—*Kol Hanishamah prayer book* Nachum Waldman

Fourth Week: *Netzah* (Persistence)

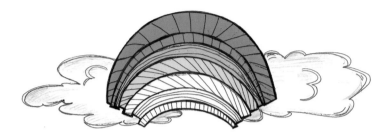

The qualities of persistence, determination, energy, and commitment are associated with *netzah*. This quality of persistence is associated with achievement and creativity; it is limitless and without boundaries. When do you feel energetic and empowered? When do you feel stuck?

During the fourth week, days 22–28 on the *Omer* chart, emphasize the soul trait of persistence *(netzah)*.

May these verses inspire your commitment to practice persistence this week.

"Let me know the road I must take" (Psalm 143)
- In breath: Let me know
- Out breath: the road I must take.

"Establish an order that shall never change" (Psalm 148)
- In breath: Establish an order
- Out breath: that shall never change.

"O preserve me, as befits your steadfast love" (Psalm 119)
- In breath: O preserve me,
- Out breath: as befits your steadfast love.

PERSONAL REFLECTIONS

Use this space to reflect on persistence and your commitment to it.

Lag B'omer

On the 33rd day of the counting of the *Omer*, we celebrate the holiday of *Lag B'omer*, a day of celebrating the joining of heaven and earth. It is a day of outdoor celebrations, bonfires, and picnics as we rejoice in the wonders of living in a created world. In this season of fire (the summer season), we remember the burning bush and the burning mountain of Sinai and invite fiery passionate expressions of gratitude, as this is the week devoted to cultivating gratitude.

Enjoy a picnic lunch outside with children.

Get a new hairstyle or haircut: Traditionally a child has a first haircut when three years old on *Lag B'omer*.

Celebrate this spring holiday with a bonfire: In Israel, the smell of acrid smoke and the glow of bonfires are everywhere on this day.

Eat a favorite food as if you are eating "manna from heaven." One tradition about *Lag B'omer* is that it was the day that the manna first fell from heaven. According to this tradition, the people of Israel finished the unleavened bread *(matzah)* that they had taken with them when they left slavery in Egypt on the 15th of Iyar (one month after *Passover*), and went hungry for three days. Then the Holy One sent down the manna, the heavenly bread, and it miraculously appeared in the wilderness. The people gathered it daily, and on Friday a double portion fell so that they did not need to gather it on the Sabbath. According to some rabbinic *midrashim*, the manna tasted like all things, any delicious thing anyone wanted to eat. The manna represents the fertility and creativity of heaven, given to the world as a Divine gift.

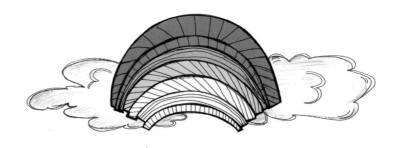

CREATE YOUR OWN MEMORIES

Use this space to jot down Omer childhood memories or something that happened this year that you want to remember—maybe a precious photo belongs here.

Fifth Week: *Hod* (Gratitude)

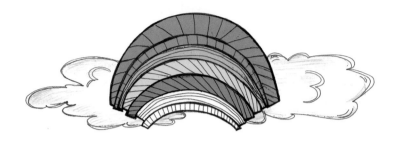

The practice of gratitude *(hod)* invites us to offer praise, give thanks, and become more aware of the blessings in our lives. Gratitude affirms. It causes us to focus on the good things in our lives and reminds us that even when things seem to be very dark and hopeless, there is something to be grateful for.

During the fifth week, days 29–35 on the *Omer* chart, emphasize the soul trait of gratitude.

May these verses inspire your commitment to practice gratitude this week.

"At midnight I will rise to give thanks to You." (Psalm 119)
- In breath: At midnight I will rise
- Out breath: to give thanks to You.

"The words You inscribed, give light." (Psalm 119)
- In breath: The words You inscribed
- Out breath: give light.

"You are the God who works wonders." (Psalm 78)
- In breath: You are the God
- Out breath: who works wonders.

Use this space to reflect on persistence and people, circumstances, and things you're grateful for in your life.

Sixth Week: *Yesod* (Composure)

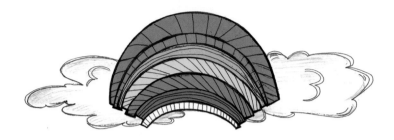

This quality, *yesod*, is about balance, about building calm and deep connections to others. This week is about the work of building a balanced life, a life of calm inner awareness and resolute composure. We want to build relationships on love, structure, and compassion. How can we build balanced lives? These verses invite you to listen to the deeper truths and possibilities of your life.

During the sixth week, days 36–42 on the *Omer* chart, focus on the soul trait of composure.

"Call upon me in time of trouble." (Psalm 50)
- In breath: Call upon me
- Out breath: in time of trouble.

"One who acts thus shall never be shaken." (Psalm 15)
- In breath: One who acts thus
- Out breath: shall never be shaken.

"Lead me on a level path." (Psalm 27)
- In breath: Lead me
- Out breath: on a level path.

PERSONAL REFLECTIONS

Use this space to reflect on balance in your life.

Seventh Week: *Mal<u>h</u>ut* (Trust)

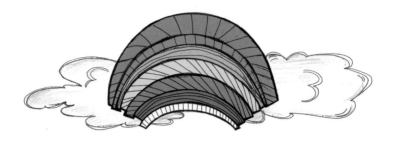

Trustworthiness begins with learning to trust others. We begin this at birth, establishing a primal trusting relationship with our caregivers. According to Erik Erikson, this relationship generates and nurtures the essential quality of trust in a human being. We thrive in a relationship of trust, holding the deepest appreciation for someone who won't let us down.

During the seventh week, days 43–50 on the *Omer* chart, concentrate on the soul trait of trust.

"You do not turn away your faithful care from me." (Psalm 66)
- In breath: You do not turn away
- Out breath: your faithful care from me.

"One who guards her tongue preserves her life." (Proverbs 13:3)
- In breath: One who guards her tongue
- Out breath: preserves her life.

"One who respects others shall himself be respected." (Proverbs 11:25)
- In breath: One who respects others
- Out breath: shall himself be respected.

PERSONAL REFLECTIONS

Use this space to evaluate this seven-week period of introspection for yourself.
What insights have you gained?

apter ELEVEN

Shavuot: Light of Torah

"The voice of Torah reaches each according to our ability to hear"
—_Midrash_

Personal Moment

Roses and Torah

On *Shavuot* a few years ago, my synagogue's Adult Confirmation class celebrated the completion of their course of study by placing long-stemmed white roses around the Torah. We traditionally decorate our homes and synagogues with plants, flowers, and leafy branches in honor of *Shavuot*. According to the *Midrash* (interpretive legend), the desert bloomed as Mount Sinai suddenly blossomed with flowers in anticipation of the giving of the Torah on its summit.

Each person uncovered a bit of the Torah (wrapped in *tallit*) as they taught some words of Torah and placed their white rose close to the sacred text of our people. The hour was late and the sanctuary was very quiet, lit only by candles and the glow on the confirmants' faces. It was a private, intimate moment of connection for each person, and the sweet scent of roses filled the air.

Years later, I can walk into the darkened sanctuary late at night and imagine that I still smell that fragrance, the fragrance of love of Torah.

PERSONAL REFLECTIONS

*Use this space to jot down Shavuot childhood memories or a favorite Torah or Bible story,
or something that happened this year that you want to remember—maybe
a precious photo belongs here.*

Meditation

Shavuot *Meditation*

Find yourself in a place of moving air. Perhaps near the ocean, on a hillside, or where gentle winds are at play in your garden.

Shavuot, the summer holiday, offers Torah to us like fragrance on the breeze in the blowing wind.

Close your eyes and breathe in the particular fragrance of this moment. Allow your sense of smell to link you to the deepest part of yourself.

Use the verse from Song of Songs—"your lips are like roses"—as you breathe in and out.

Become sensitive to the changes in the air. Notice when a new wind arrives with a new scent.

Allow yourself to be surprised by the gusts of air, the changing currents of breeze, the changes in your breath.

Encourage yourself to respond positively to change, to cultivate flexibility.

To move in the spirit of Torah, be willing to change course, to shift your present reality, to be surprised.

SPIRITUAL CHOCOLATE MOMENT

Enjoy a late night bite of chocolate. Maybe a candy bar you loved as a child— why not? The Marquise de Sevigne said, "If you are not feeling well, if you have not slept, chocolate will revive you. But you have no chocolate! My dear, how will you ever manage?"

Living by Torah's Light

Once there was a Jew who went out into the world to seek justice. He looked in the streets and the markets of cities, but could not find it. He traveled to villages and he explored distant fields and farms, but still justice eluded him. At last he came to an immense forest and he entered it, for he was certain that justice must exist somewhere within. He wandered there for many years and he saw many things—the hovels of the poorest people, the hideaways of thieves, the fine homes of corrupt politicians. And he stopped in each of these, despite the danger, and sought clues. But no one was able to help him in his quest.

One day, just as dusk was falling, he arrived at a small clay hut that looked as if it were about to collapse. Now there was something strange about this hut, for many flickering flames could be seen through the window. The man who sought justice wondered greatly about this and knocked on the door. There was no answer. He pushed the door open and entered.

Before him was a small room crowded with many shelves. On the shelves was a multitude of oil candles. Together their flames seemed to beat like wings, and the flickering light made him feel as if he were standing in the center of a quivering flame. He held up his hand and it seemed to be surrounded with an aura, and all the candles were like a constellation of stars.

Stepping closer, he saw that some of the flames burned with a very pure fire, while others were dull and still others were sputtering, about to go out. So, too, did he now notice that some of the wicks were in golden vessels, with others in silver or marble ones, while many burned in simple vessels of clay or tin.

While he stood there, marveling at that forest of candles, an old woman in a white robe came out of one of the corners and said, "*Shalom Aleichem*, my son, what are you looking for?"

"*Aleichem Shalom*," the man answered. "I have traveled everywhere searching for justice, but never have I seen anything like all these candles. Why are they burning?"

The old woman spoke softly: "Know that these are soul-candles. Each candle is the soul of one of the living. As long as it burns, the person remains alive. But when the flame burns out, he departs from life."

Then the man who sought justice turned to the old woman and asked, "Can I see the candle of *my* soul?"

The old woman led him into a corner and showed him a line of tins on a low shelf. She pointed out a small, rusty one that had very little oil left. The wick was smoking and had tilted to one side. "This is your soul," said the old woman. A great fear fell upon the man and he started to shiver. Could it be that the end of his life was so near and he did not know it?

Then the man noticed that next to his tin there was another, filled with oil. Its wick was straight, burning with a clear, pure light.

"And this one, who does it belong to?" asked the man, trembling.

"That is a secret," answered the old woman. "I only reveal each person's candle to himself alone."

Soon after that, the old woman vanished from sight, and the room seemed empty except for the candles burning on every shelf.

While the man stood there, he saw a candle on another shelf sputter and go out. For a moment, there was a wisp of smoke rising in the air, and then it was gone. One soul had just left the world.

The man's eyes returned to his own tin. He saw that only a few drops of oil remained, and he knew that the flame would soon burn out. At that instant, he saw the candle of his neighbor, burning brightly, the tin full of oil.

Suddenly, an evil thought entered his mind. He looked around and saw that the old woman had disappeared. He looked closely in the corner from which she had come, and then in the other corners, but there was no sign of her there.

At that moment, he reached out and took hold of the full tin and raised it above his own, ready to pour some oil into his own almost-empty tin. But suddenly, a strong hand gripped his arm, and the old woman stood beside him.

"Is this the kind of justice you are seeking? Is this the way you want to live your life?" Her grip was like iron, and the pain caused the man to close his eyes.

And when the fingers released him, he opened his eyes and saw that everything had disappeared: the old woman, the cottage, the shelves, and all the candles. And the man stood alone in the forest and heard the trees whispering to him.

A BISSEL (LITTLE) YIDDISH

When you say goodbye, say "ZAY geZUNT" (Be Well). In Hebrew: "Shalom" (Peace).

PERSONAL REFLECTIONS

*Use this space to jot down Shavuot childhood memories or a favorite Torah or Bible story,
or something that happened this year that you want to remember
—maybe a precious photo belongs here.*

Reflection

Shavuot is the holiday for those who travel inner journeys. Traveling with a guidebook is always easier than without one; a guidebook for life is the Torah. While the giving of the Torah is what God does on *Shavuot*, our role is to use it.

Shavuot *Reflections*

"You shall keep the Feast of Weeks to the Holy One, your God with an offering freely given from your hand, which you shall give and God shall bless you"
—*Deuteronomy 16:10*

"You shall keep the Feast of Weeks to the Holy One, your God…"
Shavuot marks the giving of the Torah at Sinai, yet the Torah never refers to this. It is described as an agricultural holiday when the first fruits of the new growing season are brought as offerings in the Temple. *Shavuot* means "weeks" because it falls on the climax of seven weeks of counting (the *omer*) until the first grain is ready. On *Shavuot* we receive the Torah, God's gift to us, the cosmic guide for how we are to live in this world.

"…with an offering freely given from your hand…"
Our offering is to truly examine ourselves, to stand with palms facing upward and commit ourselves to an inner examination. *Shavuot* is a time to take a personal assessment of the way we want to live in the world. Each of us has particular needs, questions, and longings. Each of us is on a personal journey through life.

"…which you shall give…"
What kind of personal commitment are we willing to make in accepting the Torah as our own guidebook in life? On *Shavuot*, we read the Ten Commandments from the Torah. The first five commandments remind us of our relationship to the holy, to the Holy One, to God. The second five remind us of the ways we are to treat each other. What are your Ten Commandments, the ten absolute rules that you are willing to take on yourself?

"…and God shall bless you."
The Torah is an amazing gift. Our task is to accept this blessing and to renew our commitment to Torah every day. The Torah is the answer, the guidebook, but we need to decide on the questions and choose the route so that we may travel safely and arrive at the right destinations.

Use this space to jot down the titles of favorite Jewish books or books that inspired you.

Celebration of Tradition

What to Do to Celebrate Shavuot

Light candles: We illuminate our lives by lighting candles.

Make a blessing when lighting candles on (*Shabbat* and) a holiday:

בָּרוּךְ אַתָּה יהוה אֱלֹהֵינוּ מֶלֶךְ הָעוֹלָם, אֲשֶׁר קִדְּשָׁנוּ
בְּמִצְוֹתָיו וְצִוָּנוּ לְהַדְלִיק נֵר שֶׁל (שַׁבָּת וְ) יוֹם טוֹב:

Baruh atah adonay eloheynu meleh ha'olam asher kideshanu bemitzvotav vitzivanu lehadlik ner shel (shabbat v) yom tov.
Blessed are You, Holy One, life of all worlds, who invites us to be holy and kindle the (*Shabbat* and) holiday lights.

Make a blessing over the wine–the *kiddush*:

בָּרוּךְ אַתָּה יהוה אֱלֹהֵינוּ מֶלֶךְ הָעוֹלָם בּוֹרֵא פְּרִי הַגָּפֶן:

Baruh atah adonay eloheynu meleh ha'olam borey peri hagafen.
Blessed are You, Holy One, life of all worlds, who creates the fruit of the vine.

Make a blessing over bread—the *motzi*:

בָּרוּךְ אַתָּה יהוה אֱלֹהֵינוּ מֶלֶךְ הָעוֹלָם הַמּוֹצִיא לֶחֶם
מִן הָאָרֶץ:

Baruh atah adonay eloheynu meleh ha'olam hamotzi lehem min ha'aretz.
Blessed are You, Holy One, life of all worlds, who brings forth bread from the earth.

SUGGESTED SHAVUOT MENU

Dairy meals are traditional.
Cream of mushroom soup
Salmon salad mold
Sliced cucumbers with dill
Blintz casserole
Strawberries with whipped cream

Make a blessing of gratitude—the *sheheḥeyanu*:

בָּרוּךְ אַתָּה יהוה אֱלֹהֵינוּ מֶלֶךְ הָעוֹלָם שֶׁהֶחֱיָנוּ וְקִיְּמָנוּ
וְהִגִּיעָנוּ לַזְּמַן הַזֶּה:

Baruḥ atah adonay eloheynu meleḥ ha'olam sheheḥeyanu vekiyemanu vehigi'anu lazeman hazeh.
Blessed are You, Holy One, life of all worlds, who gave us life, and kept us strong, and brought us to this time.

Make a blessing of gratitude after the meal—*birkat hamazon*—short version:

בְּרִיךְ רַחֲמָנָא מַלְכָּא דִי עָלְמָא מָרֵיהּ דְּהַאי פִּתָּא אָמֵן:

Briḥ raḥamana malka d'alma maray de hai pita. Amen.
Blessed are You, compassionate one, who provides the bread of life. Amen.

Or, if you prefer the longer version—see page 23

Decorate with greenery and flowers: Because *Shavuot* is a harvest holiday, there is a custom to decorate homes and synagogues with greenery. We also decorate with flowers, since *Shavuot* commemorates the giving of the Torah on Mount Sinai. It is said that although Mount Sinai is located in the desert, the desert bloomed with flowers when the Torah was given to the Jewish people.

Eat dairy: It is customary to eat dairy food on *Shavuot*. Some say that eating dairy shows restraint. When the Jewish people accepted the Torah and committed themselves to follow it, they committed themselves to leading lives with restraints.

Perform *Tikkun Laiyl Shavuot*: *Tikkun Laiyl Shavuot* is the custom of staying up all night long on *Shavuot* to study Torah. Studying Torah the entire night is one way to celebrate the anniversary of its giving.

Attend *Shavuot* services: It is customary for everyone, even children and infants, to attend synagogue on *Shavuot* to hear the reading of the Ten Commandments from the Torah. *Yizkor* is recited after the Torah reading on *Shavuot*.

Read from the Book of Ruth: One reason given is that Ruth's conversion is similar to the Jewish people's acceptance of the Torah. Ruth was King David's ancestor, and it is believed that King David was born and died on *Shavuot*.

Ways to Make Shavuot *Your Own*

Hold a "cosmic wedding": *Shavuot* is like a wedding between heaven and earth. On the first night of *Shavuot*, some Jews stay up all night (or at least very late) studying in a ritual called *Tikkun Laiyl Shavuot*—the repair of *Shavuot* eve. Those who study are like bridesmaids waiting up with the bride. In the morning, they accompany the bride (the Torah) to a greenery-decorated *huppah* (wedding canopy).

Celebrate with your own "cosmic wedding." Write a love letter between the Torah and Israel, between the *Shehinah* (God's presence or dwelling place) and the Holy One, and then read it as a wedding contract, a *ketubbah*.

Host a ritual for fertility and creativity: Invite friends and family to a festive meal, to a table decorated with greenery and flowers, celebrating the union of sky and earth.

Celebrate conversion: The Book of Ruth is read on *Shavuot*. Ruth represents the covenant because she chooses to be part of the people Israel out of her love for her mother-in-law Naomi. Celebrate your connection to the Jewish people and to others who have converted with a festive meal of many-grained breads (Ruth's story takes place at harvest time) and with dairy dishes.

Write a letter of thanks to God: *For example:* Dear God, Thank you for the gift of Torah. Even though we don't read the ancient Hebrew easily, these holy words are important to us. Help us to live our lives as the Torah teaches us. Help us to study more and learn more so that we may be good role models for our children and so that they may become good parents when they are ready. Help us to remember to treasure the Torah and love to be close to it.

-or-

We feel great pride in offering the Torah's Ten Commandments as a gift to the world. May the words of Torah be sweet in our mouths and linger lovingly in our hearts so that we, our children, and their children come to love you and to feel your presence in our actions and in our relationships. Give us the wisdom of Torah and teach us how to bless our world with health, abundance, joy, and peace. Amen.

PERSONAL REFLECTIONS

Take a few moments to jot down memories of family weddings (or add photos).

Blessing

A Blessing for Shavuot

During the coming week
May you enjoy good health and happiness.

May peace reign over our country
And throughout the world.

May your mind be illumined by the words of Torah
May you cling to her branches as a blossom in Spring.

May your study be passionate
As meanings reveal more meanings
and wisdom embraces you.

May Torah pour holiness into your heart
And bring warmth and comfort to your soul.

May the gift of Torah be yours to teach and
To share with your children and their children.

May the Bride of Torah enter your house with teachings of peace
And may you meet your beloved
on the streets of Jerusalem in the year to come.

Amen.

As the wilderness has no end, the Torah has no end
—Midrash

The world exists because Israel accepts the Torah
—Midrash

The word reached each one,
according to their ability to hear
—Midrash

As between each large wave in the sea there are small
waves, as between each word of Torah are all
its details and interpretations
—Midrash

REPAIR THE WORLD: TZEDAKAH OPPORTUNITY

*On **Shavuot** we celebrate the joys of receiving Torah, of being known as the People of the Book. This holiday offers you the opportunity to help others enjoy the miracle of literacy. Perhaps you (along with family and friends) will help someone learn to read. Or you may help supply books or volunteer at your local library. One national Jewish organization that responds: Koreh L.A., www.jewishla.org*

chapter *TWELVE*

ROSH HODESH: CYCLE OF RENEWAL

"Renew this month for us, for goodness and for blessing"
—*Siddur*

Rosh Hodesh *for Love*

It was a big year for me—and as *Rosh Hodesh Heshvan* coincided with my October birthday, I decided to throw a *Rosh Hodesh* party for myself. I invited everyone in my *Rosh Hodesh* group to bring a candle and a blessing, and I would provide the champagne and chocolate. I was turning 50, I'd just moved into the first home I'd ever bought entirely by myself, and year-old memories of chemotherapy and radiation were fading fast.

The evening was lovely and the candlelight cast a flattering light on all our faces, drawing us into a sacred circle of women. We shared some stories, read some poetry, and laughed a lot. Just as the evening was drawing to a close, my friends announced they had a special gift for me. Because the gift was one that needed my active involvement, I had to agree to participate before they would unwrap their surprise.

They had gotten together and written a personal ad for me that was to run in *The Exponent*, Philadelphia's Jewish newspaper. My part was to have a coffee with anyone interesting who responded to the ad. A few weeks later, those responding to my *Rosh Hodesh* gift began to leave messages on my phone. The first (and only) man I met for coffee, Bob, turned out to be the man who would follow me to Pacific Palisades, California, and into my heart. He was the man who would become my husband.

PERSONAL REFLECTIONS

Use this space to jot down important or inspiring memories of women who influenced your life.

Meditation

Rosh Hodesh *Meditation*

Devote this evening, when no moon is visible in the night sky, to rest and personal renewal.

Make a sacred circle of space for yourself. Surround yourself with small votive lights, arranged in a circle around your chair or cushion.

Step into your sacred circle, into a space of renewal and nourishment.

Invite the renewal of the new moon and the new month into your life.

Ask for physical health and radiance.

Ask for blessings of goodness and joy.

Invite compassion to temper your life so that you may blossom as you age.

Promise to encourage creativity, strength, and serenity within and without.

Bless yourself with satisfaction, success, and sustenance.

Know that these blessings are yours and will always be yours.

Sip wine. Eat chocolate. Rub lotion on your feet.

As you leave your sacred circle, breathe the blessings of the moon, she who retreats in order to emerge whole, into your heart.

SPIRITUAL CHOCOLATE MOMENT

Indulge in an exquisite piece of chocolate—one of those decorated pieces of fine chocolate that were never meant to be shared. **Rosh Hodesh** *invites indulgence. As Sandra Boynton, writes in* **Chocolate: The Consuming Passion,** *"Dark chocolate is more straightforward, less playful than milk chocolate. Those who favor dark chocolate have little patience with cute candy."*

PERSONAL REFLECTIONS

Take a few moments to jot down ideas or things you've experimented with to make this holiday meaningful for you: recipes, something someone said that touched you, a promise or hope that you want to journal about....

The Queen's Yearning

Once there was a queen who reigned in a land of perfect harmony where everything went well. There was always rain at the right time. The crops were abundant. Everyone worked well with each other. No one quarreled.

This harmony flowed from the queen, for she knew everything that happened in her realm, the nature of each of her subjects. She knew when to speak forcefully, and when to be gentle and kind. She knew the land and the seas, the seasons, winds, and currents. She knew how to measure and how to weigh.

She also knew herself, and she recognized a strong yearning that came from a place deep within her. "Perhaps if I learn to sing, I will satisfy this yearning," she thought. So she learned to sing. She studied for years, and finally she sang for her subjects and they all praised her singing. No matter what she sang, they praised her. All of her songs were greeted with the same delight and praise. Yet her yearning was not satisfied. "Perhaps I do sing well," the queen thought. "Perhaps not. I will never improve because I never get honest criticism. My subjects love me too much."

So she tried to satisfy her yearning by learning to dance. She studied and finally danced before her subjects. All praised her dancing. No matter what she danced, they praised her. All her dances were greeted with the same delight and praise.

Her yearning was not satisfied.

She became an artisan, a great glass blower. She studied and worked hard and showed her subjects a glass globe that seemed to fold into itself. It was so beautiful that it took one's breath away. All who saw it praised it, and with the praise, the globe resonated and finally shattered. Her subjects were shocked. "It's all right," she reassured them, and made another. This globe was more beautiful than the first. Again, all who saw it praised it, and again the globe resonated with the praise and shattered. She made another, and it met the same fate. Word spread of the beauty and frailty of the queen's globes. To praise them was to destroy them.

All this time the queen was busy shaping her fourth globe, a fabrication of beauty beyond words. At last she announced to the people it was ready and all might come to see it, but no one came. No one dared to come. All were afraid to come. So the queen's most wonderful creation existed by itself with none to see it except the queen herself.

She poured all her yearning into the globe. Day after day, she opened her heart into it, until the globe began to glow and shimmer with a light of its own. The light grew and pulsed and finally this globe, too, shattered.

The cry that went out from the queen's palace was so great and filled with such anguish that everyone in the realm shuddered and hid. The queen had never known a loss like this. She turned into herself in mourning.

For a week, she mourned. For a week, the sharp fragments of the shattered globe lay untouched. At the end of the week, the queen herself went to remove the pieces. When she bent over, she saw to her astonishment that each shard contained some of the light of her yearning. The globe had shattered into thousands of pieces, but each piece, no matter how small, no matter what shape, contained some of that light.

The queen didn't know what to do. To sweep them up and throw them away was unthinkable. To rearrange them was also unthinkable. She was afraid that if she so much as touched one, the delicate balance that sustained the light would be destroyed. All that would be left would be pieces of broken glass.

So the queen kept her distance, and continued yearning toward the pieces of her creation, the pieces that contained her light. Over time she noticed that, with a will of their own, the pieces slowly moved toward each other and established bonds.

The queen was patient, her yearning constant. As each piece joined another, her joy increased.

Reflections

Rosh Hodesh, a minor holiday for all traditional Jews, has become a force for spiritual creativity and cultural change. The renewal of the moon, when the moon begins to show its light after a dark period, is a day for Jews to celebrate our own renewal.

Rosh Hodesh *Reflections*

In the prayer book we read:

"May the blessed Holy One renew this month for us and for all who dwell on earth, a life in which our heart's petitions are fulfilled for goodness."
—Seder Birkat Hahodesh/Blessing of the New Month

"May the blessed Holy One renew this month..."
The Jewish calendar, unlike the secular calendar, is arranged according to the phases of the moon. Many Jewish festivals fall on the full moon. *Rosh Hodesh* (literally, "head of the month" or "head of the moon"), the first of every Hebrew month, always falls on the new moon. In biblical times, *Rosh Hodesh* was a festival marked by celebratory sacrifice and feasting. In rabbinic times, bonfires were lit on the mountains to announce the arrival of the new moon.

"...for us..."
How did *Rosh Hodesh* become a women's holiday? The *Midrash* (interpretive legend) from the rabbinic period (4th–10th century) comments on the story of the Golden Calf, when the Israelite nation made and worshipped a gold idol while Moses was receiving the Torah on Mount Sinai:

"The women heard about the making of the Golden Calf and refused to give their jewelry to their husbands. Instead, they said to them: 'You want to construct an idol, a molten form which is an abomination? We won't listen to you!' And the Holy One of Blessing rewarded them in this world that they would observe the new moons more than men, and in the next world they are destined to be renewed like the moon..."
—Pirkei de Rabbi Eliezer, 45

A BISSEL (LITTLE) YIDDISH

Say "GUT KHOYdesh" (A Good Month). In Hebrew: "Hodesh Tov" (A Good Month).

In this interpretation, the women are rewarded with a holiday because of their independence, wisdom, and piety in the face of an inappropriate request. *Rosh* *Hodesh* becomes a celebration of women's commitment to the Israelite vision of God.

"...and for all who dwell on earth..."
A variety of colorful sources tells us how women celebrated *Rosh* *Hodesh* in different time periods. There was a widespread custom for women not to work on the new moon. Women refrained from spinning, weaving, cleaning, and other difficult chores. Although some felt women should not entirely refrain from work (in order not to embarrass men), women were encouraged to abstain from all but light work. Some women lit memorial candles on *Rosh* *Hodesh*. In Yemen, candles were lit in homes and synagogues, and in Algiers, gold coins would be placed inside the burning candles for good luck. In Europe, Ashkenazic women recited special Yiddish prayers called techinas for *Rosh* *Hodesh*, and some women collected charity for the poor. Jewish women even used the holiday to entertain themselves with gambling.

"...a life in which our heart's petitions..."
Today, *Rosh* *Hodesh* celebrations include new music and prayer as well as re-creations of old rituals. Some groups gather to celebrate biblical women and tell new stories about them. Others gather to explore Jewish law and practice. Some groups invent ways to worship feminine aspects of divinity, or to celebrate new rites of passage related to women's lives. Many new women's rituals come out of *Rosh* *Hodesh* communities. Members of *Rosh* *Hodesh* groups come from all religious denominations and levels of observance.

"...are fulfilled for goodness."
We find fulfillment when we make a space for ourselves to restore, refresh, and renew ourselves. *Rosh* *Hodesh* offers a space away, a time to come home to who we really are, to sing of our journeys and tell our stories, and to laugh and stretch and renew as does the moon. The new moon, a dark time when we wait and hope for the moon's light, has now become a symbol of women celebrating our rightful place in Jewish tradition.

Celebration of Tradition

What to Do to Celebrate Rosh H̲odesh

Rosh H̲odesh means different things to different women. Some light a candle, make a blessing over a cup honoring Miriam the prophet, or buy flowers. Some attend an independent group; others attend a synagogue-affiliated *Rosh H̲odesh* group. Some *Rosh H̲odesh* groups focus on study of Torah or other texts, or invite a woman speaker or teacher. Some discuss current events, women's history, or their own spiritual struggles. Some focus on inventing creative new rituals; some just begin or end with a ritual. Many groups focus on life events, activities, or themes pertaining to the month: new growth for Shvat, the month of the trees' birthday; mourning for *Av*, month of the destruction of the Temple; masks and hiding for *Adar*, the month of *Purim*; freedom for *Nisan*, the month of *Passover*. Some groups work on art projects or other creative work that centers on women and Judaism.

Say a prayer for lighting a candle of the new moon:

בָּרוּךְ אַתָּה יהוה הַמְקַדֵּשׁ אוֹתָנוּ וּמְחַדֵּשׁ אוֹתָנוּ עַל יְדֵי
הַדְלָקַת נֵר שֶׁל רֹאשׁ חֹדֶשׁ:

Baruh̲ ata Yah hamekadesh otanu umeh̲adesh otanu al yadei hadlakat ner shel Rosh H̲odesh.
Blessed are You, Holy One, who consecrates us and renews us through the lighting of the fires of Rosh H̲odesh.

Say a blessing over bread, the "Bread of Our Souls":

בָּרוּכָה אַתּ יָה שְׁכִינָה הַמּוֹצִיאָה לֶחֶם שֶׁל נִשְׁמוֹתֵּנוּ:

Bruh̲a Yah Sheh̲inah hamotziah leh̲em shel nishmotanu.
Blessed is Sheh̲inah who brings forth the bread of our souls.

Sheh̲inah, like bread,
Is manna to our souls.
She feeds us renewal
The substance of life.

SUGGESTED ROSH H̲ODESH MENU

Wine tasting
Cheese tasting
Cookie tasting

CREATE YOUR OWN MEMORIES

Use this space to jot down important months and dates—birthdays, anniversaries, or other important moments on the calendar.

New Rituals

Ways to Make Rosh <u>H</u>odesh *Your Own*

Perform a naming of yourself and of your matriarchs: Go around the room counterclockwise (as the moon travels), naming each person. This may be done in English, Hebrew, Ladino, Yiddish, or any other language. The matrilineal line may extend as far as each woman is able.

I am _____ daughter of _____ daughter of _____ daughter of _____ and on and on.

TOGETHER: We welcome *Rosh <u>H</u>odesh* _____ (fill in the month).

We welcome our ancestors, the matriarchs Sarah, Rebecca, Leah, and Rachel.

From the East, we call to our sister Sarah, daughter of Mesopotamia, princess and honored one. Sarah, the first matriarch, joins us from the place where the sun rises, the place to which we Jews turn. Mother of beginnings, join us now as we come together to celebrate the cycles of time and change.

From the West, we call to our sister Rebecca, daughter of the well. Rebecca, woman of tenacity and courage, joins us from the land where the sun sets. Mother of contractions and contradictions, join us now as we come together to celebrate the cycles of time and change.

From the North, we call to our sister Leah, tender-eyed and inward-looking. Leah, who learned to live with less, joins us from the fertile north, the land of green and deep running streams. Mother of patience and fortitude, join us now as we come together to celebrate the cycles of time and change.

From the South, we call to our sister Rachel, whose love was stronger than death. Rachel joins us from the place where heat is intense, the light blinding, the truth searing. Mother of pleasure and pain, join us now as we come together to celebrate the cycles of time and change.

CREATE YOUR OWN MEMORIES

Use this space to jot down memories of birthdays, anniversaries,
or other important moments on the calendar.

GARDENING FOR THE SOUL: GATHER FLOWERS

Gather a bouquet of the freshest flowers in your garden in celebration of the time of the new moon. When no moon can be seen in the night sky, Rosh Hodesh is very close. Bring your attention to the waning of the Moon as a reminder to gather your monthly bouquet with reverence, wonder, and joy.

For each month, you might gather a group of women together and celebrate as described below:

Tevet, Moon of returning light: *Rosh Hodesh Tevet* is the seventh day of Hanukah and is celebrated as the day to remember Judith, the heroine who beheaded the wicked Holofernes. We tell the stories about the descent of heroines to the underworld in search of new wisdom.

Shevat, Moon of the sap rising in the trees: During *Shevat* we celebrate the new year of the trees, and the tree as a symbol of our people. As the sap rises and the light returns, we tell stories of pioneer women who blossomed early and cleared paths for us to follow.

Adar, Moon of Queen Esther: *Adar* is the time we celebrate the story of Queen Esther, who revealed her true identity to the king in order to save her people. We remember Persian and other Middle Eastern women's traditions with belly dancing, drumming, and feasting, and we tell stories about women who saved lives.

Nisan, Liberation Moon: This is the season of our freedom. We remember the women of the Exodus generation and tell stories about women who struggle for justice.

Iyar, Journey Moon: We tell the story of our wanderings in the wilderness in search of the proverbial promised land, and how we healed ourselves from old wounds to make ready for new revelations.

Sivan, Moon of revelations: *Sivan* is the month we received the Torah on Mount Sinai, both the written and oral tradition. During *Sivan* we share stories and wisdom from women in Jewish tradition.

Tammuz, **Moon of premonitions:** This is the moon when the first brick in the wall protecting the Temple in Jerusalem was removed from its foundation, which was the first step toward its destruction. We tell stories about someone's premonitions as a source of wisdom.

Av, **Moon of the vine dance:** *Av* is the moon when wealthier women exchanged white garments with poor women so the very poor would be dressed in the garments of the rich. The women went out into the fields to dance among the grapevines, calling upon and renewing the beauty within. We tell stories of women who walk in beauty even in times of trouble.

Elul, **Moon of "I am to my beloved as my beloved is to me":** We prepare ourselves for the new year of the soul by creating amulets that bear the sign of protection and strength for us. Then we learn to blow the *shofar*!

Tishri, **Moon of balances:** This is the national holy day of all the people. Women can celebrate *Rosh Hodesh* on the evening of the second day, if there is the opportunity to do so. We go to the *shvitz* and sweat for the new year to purify our feminine nature.

Heshvan, **Flood Moon:** We celebrate the *yahrtzeit* (death anniversary) of Rachel and tell flood tales. We meditate on the meaning of water in our lives and learn to use a *mikveh*.

Kislev, **Moon of rededication:** This is the time we reconsecrate our life to the keeping of the ways of our people, even as we invest old symbols with new meaning. We tell stories of women who helped us stay connected to our culture.

Blessing

A Blessing for Rosh Hodesh

During the coming month
May you enjoy good health and happiness.

May peace reign over our country
And throughout the world.

May you awaken to the mystery of being here
And enter the quiet palace of your own presence.

May you receive great encouragement when new opportunities arise.
May you respond to the call of your gift and find the courage to follow its path.

May you take time to celebrate the quiet miracles that seek no attention.
May you experience this coming month as a sacred gift woven around the
heart of wonder.

May the new moon enter your heart with lessons of constant cycles of return.

May you meet your beloved on the streets of Jerusalem in the year to come.

Amen.

Because of the merit of women, Israel was redeemed
from Egypt
—Midrash

O Divine One, Pray heal her
—Numbers 12:13

What a lioness was your mother among the lions
—Ezekiel 19:2

Why was the moon created? For seasons, so that
we might renew by her countings the new moons
and the years...
—Midrash

chapter *THIRTEEN*

MEMORY: YIZKOR AND YAHRTZEIT, HOLOCAUST REMEMBRANCE DAY (YOM HASHOAH)

One generation goes,
Another comes,
But the earth remains the same forever.
The sun rises and the sun sets,
And glides back to where it rises.
Southward blowing, turning northward, ever turning blows the wind,
On its rounds the wind returns.
All streams flow into the sea,
Yet the sea is never full.
To the place from which they flow,
The streams flow back again.

—*Ecclesiastes 1:4–7*

Yizkor

Observed on *Yom Kippur* afternoon, and on the morning of the last days of *Sukkot*, *Passover*, and on *Shavuot*, we remember those whose love sustained us in the past and whose memories sustain us now. Jewish tradition teaches that between the living and the dead we find a window, not a wall.

Yizkor creates a sacred time and space, inviting us to open our hearts and minds to the possibility of a true connection with those who have left behind the world of the living. Remember to ask for and offer forgiveness even with those no longer with us, forgiving them for hurts we still carry and asking forgiveness for hurts we have caused.

If we can do nothing else, then we should forgive ourselves for the burdens we carry. We bring this same awareness each year on the anniversary of the death of a loved one, known as the *yahrtzeit*.

Light a *Yizkor* candle: Available at almost every food store, a simple *yahrtzeit* candle that burns for the entire 24 hours of the day of remembrance is lit as *Kaddish* is said. Light the candle at dusk before the day when the *Yizkor* service takes place. A candle is also lit on the anniversary *(yahrtzeit)* of a loved one's death.

Say *Kaddish*:

יִתְגַּדַּל וְיִתְקַדַּשׁ שְׁמֵהּ רַבָּא בְּעָלְמָא דִּי בְרָא כִרְעוּתֵהּ וְיַמְלִיךְ מַלְכוּתֵהּ בְּחַיֵּיכוֹן וּבְיוֹמֵיכוֹן וּבְחַיֵּי דְכָל בֵּית יִשְׂרָאֵל בַּעֲגָלָא וּבִזְמַן קָרִיב וְאִמְרוּ אָמֵן:

יְהֵא שְׁמֵהּ רַבָּא מְבָרַךְ לְעָלַם וּלְעָלְמֵי עָלְמַיָּא:

יִתְבָּרַךְ וְיִשְׁתַּבַּח וְיִתְפָּאַר וְיִתְרוֹמַם וְיִתְנַשֵּׂא וְיִתְהַדָּר וְיִתְעַלֶּה וְיִתְהַלַּל שְׁמֵהּ דְּקֻדְשָׁא בְּרִיךְ הוּא לְעֵלָּא (לְעֵלָּא) (On Shabbat Shuvah, add:) מִן כָּל בִּרְכָתָא וְשִׁירָתָא תֻּשְׁבְּחָתָא וְנֶחֱמָתָא דַּאֲמִירָן בְּעָלְמָא וְאִמְרוּ אָמֵן: יְהֵא שְׁלָמָא רַבָּא מִן שְׁמַיָּא וְחַיִּים עָלֵינוּ וְעַל כָּל יִשְׂרָאֵל וְאִמְרוּ אָמֵן:

עוֹשֶׂה שָׁלוֹם בִּמְרוֹמָיו הוּא יַעֲשֶׂה שָׁלוֹם עָלֵינוּ וְעַל כָּל יִשְׂרָאֵל וְעַל כָּל יוֹשְׁבֵי תֵבֵל וְאִמְרוּ אָמֵן:

Yitgadal veyitkadash shemey raba be'alma divra ḥirutey veyamliḥ malḥutey beḥayeyḥon uvyomeyḥon uvḥayey deḥol beyt yisra'el ba'agala uvizman kariv ve'imru amen.

Yeḥey shemey raba mevaraḥ le'olam ulelmey almaya.

Yitbaraḥ veyishtabaḥ veyitpa'ar veyitromam veyitnasey veyit-hadar veyi-taleḥ veyit-halal shemey dekudsha beriḥ hu le'ela (On Shabbat Shuvah add: le'ela) min kol birḥata veshirata tushbeḥata veneḥemata da'amiran be'alma ve'imru amen.

Yeḥey shelama raba min shemaya veḥayim aleynu ve'al kol yisra'el ve'imru amen. Oseh shalom bimromav hu ya'aseh shalom aleynu ve'al kol yisra'el ve'al kol yoshvey tevel ve'imru amen.

Let God's name be made great and holy in the world that was created as God willed. May God complete the holy realm in your own lifetime, in your days, and in the days of all the house of Israel, quickly and soon. And say: Amen.

May God's great name be blessed, forever and as long as worlds endure.

May it be blessed, and praised, and glorified, and held in honor, viewed with awe, embellished, and revered; and may the blessed name of holiness be hailed, though it be higher (*On Shabbat Shuvah add:* by far) than all the blessings, songs, praises, and consolations that we utter in this world. And say: Amen.

May Heaven grant a universal peace, and life for us, and for all Israel. And say: Amen.

May the one who creates harmony above, make peace for us and for all Israel, and for all who dwell on earth. And say: Amen.

Attend the *Yizkor* service: This short memorial service involves both a commemoration of death and a quest for a higher level of spirituality.

Visit the cemetery: It is an appropriate time to visit the graves of loved ones.

Share this poem:

Death Is Always Personal

Death is always personal.
We filter our pain through the memories of loss
felt and held in the recesses of our hearts
and the fiber of our beings.
As tears beget tears,
and sighs birth shuddering sighs,
we make meaning of tragedy and loss
in small and personal ways.
Death is always personal.

And the personal is our reality,
what we know to be real and true.
Each of us has our own precious memories,
the look of a loving smile, scent of sweet perfume,
taste of shared pleasure, feel of an all-enveloping hug,
sound of a well-remembered laugh.
Death is always personal.

Our personal losses do not isolate us,
we share the miracle of being human
comforted by the shared companionship of those around us.
When we open our hearts to our own personal memories,
we are embraced by community,
the community of all those who have suffered and lost.
One shared sigh, one common cry, one rhythm of release.

Communal yearnings link us to each other,
common dreams and connected longings recognize our shared humanity.
We are all one—in our pain, in our grief, in our tender suffering.
We can take solace and support from the presence of others,
the comfort and compassion of living in community,
acknowledging death is always personal.

Yom HaShoah, Holocaust Memorial Day

During the second week of the *Omer*, on the 12th day of the Omer, is Holocaust Memorial Day, *Yom HaShoah*. We remember an ancient story about the way the Holy One felt when so many people died at the Red Sea.

Once there was a wise leader, a wonderful king, whose children were captured, enslaved, and some of them died. The king rejoiced with all those who could be saved, the ones who were left, the ones who survived. But the joy was incomplete. No one could comfort this wise leader for all the lost children. Our rabbis teach that God is this wise leader. Our rabbis teach that "the Holy One was not comforted." The Holy One rejoiced and welcomed all those who could be saved. But, like the wise leader, no matter how happy the king was because of those who lived, the Holy One could not be comforted for those who had died.

This story does not explain why suffering happens, nor why so many died, but evokes an image of a Holy One who is all too human, having arrived too late to save the murdered. Like us, the Holy One grieves for those who have been lost. As Jews, we remember the victims of the Holocaust and promise to derive meaning from such horror by working for the end of suffering for all people.

Light a *yahrtzeit* candle: Some people light six candles, one for each million of the six million souls who perished during the Holocaust.

Memorial Prayer for *Yom HaShoah*

On this night we kindle light to remember the Jewish lives that were snuffed out.

As we kindle this light, we remember the lights of the Jewish homes and synagogues all over Europe that were extinguished during the tragic years of the *Shoah*. Darkness covered the Jewish world.

On this night we recall those whose love and courage brought glimmers of light through the darkness.

On this night we kindle a Jewish light in our home. We kindle it with hope and with a promise to bring light to all who still sit in darkness.

...continued on page 230

Light the *yahrtzeit* candle(s) here.

I believe in the sun even when it is not shining.
I believe in love even when not feeling it.
I believe in God even when God is silent.
   —*found in a letter in Cologne where Jews had hidden from the Nazis*

Say Kaddish (see page 226).

Make a special effort to hear the story of any Holocaust survivors (or children of survivors) that you know: Personal stories keep memory alive. In the Talmud we read "God created people because God loves stories."

Attend a *Yom HaShoah* Memorial Service.

Share your family's Jewish genealogy and stories: If nothing else, write down the names of your mother, grandmother, and great-grandmother, and go as far back as you can. Do the same for your father, grandfather, etc. Write their names (and any anecdotal information you have) on the following pages. Family records can be recorded and remembered. After all, as Elie Wiesel teaches, "Memory is the only thing we ever really own."

For love is as strong as death,
passion as might as life's end,
its flames are flames of fire,
a blaze of God.
—*Song of Songs 8:6*

Do not hand me over to the Angel of Death.
A Heavenly voice said, "Do not be afraid.
I myself will see to you."
—*Midrash*

PERSONAL FAMILY GENEALOGY

Mother's Family

_____

Father's Family

_____

YOUR FAMILY RECORDS

Births

Names	Date of Birth	Hebrew Date

Deaths

Names	Date of Birth	Hebrew Date

Marriages

Names	Date of Marriage	Hebrew Date

Jewish Holidays Calendar

Holidays are celebrated on the same day of the Jewish calendar every year, but the Jewish year is not the same length as a solar year on the Gregorian calendar used by most of the western world, so the date shifts on the Gregorian calendar.

The Jewish calendar is based on three astronomical phenomena: the rotation of the earth about its axis (a day); the revolution of the moon about the earth (a month); and the revolution of the earth about the sun (a year). The Gregorian calendar used by most of the world has abandoned any correlation between the moon cycles and the month, arbitrarily setting the length of months to 28, 30, or 31 days.

The Jewish calendar, however, coordinates all three of these astronomical phenomena. Months are either 29 or 30 days, corresponding to the 29-day lunar cycle. Years are either 12 or 13 months, corresponding to the 12.4-month solar cycle.

In the fourth century, Hillel II established a fixed calendar based on mathematical and astronomical calculations. This calendar, still in use, standardized the length of months and the addition of months over the course of a 19-year cycle, so that the lunar calendar realigns with the solar years. Jewish holidays follow the Jewish calendar. For dates of upcoming Jewish holidays, see below.

2008–2009 (5769)

All Jewish holidays begin at sundown on the evening before the date shown.

Rosh Hashanah: 30 September 2008 *(Tuesday)*
Yom Kippur: 9 October 2008 *(Thursday)*
Sukkot: 14 October 2008 *(Tuesday)*
Simhat Torah: 22 October 2008 *(Wednesday)*
Hanukah: 22 December 2008 *(Monday)*
Tu Bishvat: 9 February 2009 *(Monday)*
Purim: 10 March 2009 *(Tuesday)*
Passover (Pesah): 9 April 2009 *(Thursday)*
Holocaust Remembrance Day *(Yom HaShoah)*: 21 April 2009 *(Tuesday)*
Israel Independence Day *(Yom HaAtzmaut)*: 29 April 2009 *(Wednesday)*
Lag B'omer: 12 May 2009 *(Tuesday)*
Shavuot: 29 May 2009 *(Friday)*
Tisha B'av: 30 July 2009 *(Thursday)*

2009–2010 (5770)

All Jewish holidays begin at sundown on the evening before the date shown.

Rosh Hashanah: 19 September 2009 *(Saturday)*
Yom Kippur: 28 September 2009 *(Monday)*
Sukkot: 3 October 2009 *(Saturday)*
Simḥat Torah: 11 October 2009 *(Sunday)*
Hanukah: 12 December 2009 *(Saturday)*
Tu Bishvat: 30 January 2010 *(Saturday)*
Purim: 28 February 2010 *(Sunday)*
Passover (Pesaḥ): 30 March 2010 *(Tuesday)*
Holocaust Remembrance Day *(Yom HaShoah)*: 11 April 2010 *(Sunday)*
Israel Independence Day *(Yom HaAtzmaut)*: 19 April 2010 *(Monday)*
Lag B'omer: 2 May 2010 *(Sunday)*
Shavuot: 19 May 2010 *(Wednesday)*
Tisha B'av: 20 July 2010 *(Tuesday)*

2010–2011 (5771)

All Jewish holidays begin at sundown on the evening before the date shown.

Rosh Hashanah: 9 September 2010 *(Thursday)*
Yom Kippur: 18 September 2010 *(Saturday)*
Sukkot: 23 September 2010 *(Thursday)*
Simḥat Torah: 1 October 2010 *(Friday)*
Hanukah: 2 December 2010 *(Thursday)*
Tu Bishvat: 20 January 2011 *(Thursday)*
Purim: 20 March 2011 *(Sunday)*
Passover (Pesaḥ): 19 April 2011 *(Tuesday)*
Holocaust Remembrance Day *(Yom HaShoah)*: 1 May 2011 *(Sunday)*
Israel Independence Day *(Yom HaAtzmaut)*: 9 May 2011 *(Monday)*
Lag B'omer: 22 May 2011 *(Sunday)*
Shavuot: 8 June 2011 *(Wednesday)*
Tisha B'av: 9 August 2011 *(Tuesday)*

2011–2012 (5772)

All Jewish holidays begin at sundown on the evening before the date shown.

Rosh Hashanah: 29 September 2011 *(Thursday)*
Yom Kippur: 8 October 2011 *(Saturday)*
Sukkot: 13 October 2011 *(Thursday)*
Simhat Torah: 21 October 2011 *(Friday)*
Hanukah: 21 December 2011 *(Wednesday)*
Tu Bishvat: 8 February 2012 *(Wednesday)*
Purim: 8 March 2012 *(Thursday)*
Passover (Pesah): 7 April 2012 *(Saturday)*
Holocaust Remembrance Day *(Yom HaShoah)*: 19 April 2012 *(Thursday)*
Israel Independence Day *(Yom HaAtzmaut)*: 26 April 2012 *(Thursday)*
Lag B'omer: 10 May 2012 *(Thursday)*
Shavuot: 27 May 2012 *(Sunday)*
Tisha B'av: 29 July 2012 *(Sunday)*

2012–2013 (5773)

All Jewish holidays begin at sundown on the evening before the date shown.

Rosh Hashanah: 17 September 2012 *(Monday)*
Yom Kippur: 26 September 2012 *(Wednesday)*
Sukkot: 1 October 2012 *(Monday)*
Simhat Torah: 9 October 2012 *(Tuesday)*
Hanukah: 9 December 2012 *(Sunday)*
Tu Bishvat: 26 January 2013 *(Saturday)*
Purim: 24 February 2013 *(Sunday)*
Passover (Pesah): 26 March 2013 *(Tuesday)*
Holocaust Remembrance Day *(Yom HaShoah)*: 7 April 2013 *(Sunday)*
Israel Independence Day *(Yom HaAtzmaut)*: 15 April 2013 *(Monday)*
Lag B'omer: 28 April 2013 *(Sunday)*
Shavuot: 15 May 2013 *(Wednesday)*
Tisha B'av: 16 July 2013 *(Tuesday)*

CREATE YOUR OWN MEMORIES

Use this space to jot down important months and dates—birthdays, anniversaries, or other important moments on the calendar.

About Rabbi Sheryl Lewart

Sheryl Lewart is a spiritual teacher who lectures and leads workshops and seminars in Mystical Judaism (Kabbalah, Hasidism, and Mussar). She serves as a rabbi of Kehillat Israel, the largest Reconstructionist congregation in the world, serving more than 1,000 households, in Los Angeles, California, and gives seminars regularly on values-based decision-making.

After graduating from Cornell University with a bachelor of science in child development and family relationships, she taught school in a rural Mennonite community near Philadelphia while studying for her master's degree in education at Lehigh University.

As an entrepreneur, she owned both an antiques business and a custom rug weaving business near New Hope, Pennyslvania, before beginning her rabbinical studies at the Reconstructionist Rabbinical College in Philadelphia. As part of her study, she lived in Jerusalem for a year while attending Hebrew University, and she was ordained in 1994, graduating with a master's degree in Hebrew Letters. From 1994 to 1998, she was Director of Outreach for the Jewish Reconstructionist Federation.

She is a founding rabbinic cohort member of the Institute for Jewish Spirituality, which is dedicated to exploring, renewing, and applying the riches of Jewish spiritual traditions in order to enrich the inner lives of Jews and, ultimately, link the search for inner wholeness with social and environmental activism. She is also a member of Spiritual Directors International, whose calling it is to support and encourage holiness around the world and across spiritual traditions.

Having studied Spiritual Formation at the Mercy Center in Burlingame, California, Sheryl now offers spiritual direction and guidance in order to help others understand that by developing our own spirituality, we discover a deeper intimacy with God and a genuine compassion for all of creation. God, it has been suggested, is the wind that blows our ship, but it is up to us to turn the rudder and shift the sails in order to more fully catch the wind that freely blows.

In addition to her many other activities, Sheryl has been an adjunct faculty member of the Reconstructionist Rabbinical College; was the editor of *Jewish, Alive & American*, an innovative introduction to Judaism and conversion course in national distribution; has written a column for *The Jewish Exponent* (Philadelphia); and has been published in Reconstructionism Today and *The Jewish Journal* (Los Angeles).

She is a mother and grandmother, and lives with her husband, Bob, in Los Angeles, California.

change happens

Printed in Canada
By Friesens

Subsidiary Production Office
Santa Rosa, CA, USA
888.340.6049

ISBN 978-0-615-26226-0

Kehillat Israel Reconstructionist Congregation
16019 Sunset Boulevard, Pacific Palisades, CA 90272
www.kehillatisrael.org